MAINSTREAMING OF SCHOOL DROPOUTS: A STUDY IN KURNOOL DISTRICT OF ANDHRA PRADESH

By

M.SUDHA PARIMALA

Create Space-Amazon Publications
4900 LaCross Road
North Charleston, SC 29406
USA
www.createspace.com

MAINSTREAMING OF SCHOOL DROPOUTS: A STUDY IN KURNOOL DISTRICT OF ANDHRA PRADESH

Published by:

Create Space-Amazon Publications
4900 LaCross Road
North Charleston, SC 29406
USA
www.createspace.com

First Edition- 2016

ISBN : 9781541027046

Price : 400/-

2016, Authors:

Create space - Amazon Publications

ACKNOWLEDGEMENTS

I deem it a great privilege to place on record, with profound respect, my sense of gratitude to my Research Supervisor, Dr.G.Sreedhar, Professor Department of Rural Development and Social Work, S.K.University, Anantapur for her scholarly academic guidance and thought provoking insights in research pursuits. Indeed, I am benefited immensely with his illuminating ideas on social science research, which instilled in me an earnest zeal to learn various domains of rural development. Above all, he has extended all possible moral support, inspiring encouragement, and showed a heap of love and affection for the completion of my research work. I owe him forever. I am equally thankful to his family members for their affectionate hospitality.

I earnestly pay my humble obeisance to my beloved parents who nursed and nurtured, showered their blessings, inspired and helped me in all endeavours although.

I take it as privilege to express my thanks to **Prof.D.Chenna Reddy;** Chairman, Board of Studies, Department of Rural Development and Social Work and the authorities of Sri Krishnadevaraya University, for providing the necessary facilities for completion of the work.

I record my heart-felt gratitude to **Prof.V.Reddappa Reddy, Prof.K.Bhaskar, Prof.C. Sudhakar, Prof.R.Suguna Kumari, (Retd) Prof.Late. K.Govindappa, Prof.M.Muninarayanappa, Dr.P.Firoz Babu,** Assistant Professor; **Dr.D.Sreenivasa Reddy,** Teaching Personnel, Department of Rural Development and Social Work, S.K.University, Ananthapuramu, for their inspiration, encouragement and moral support extended throughout my research work.

I express my special sincere thanks to the officials of NCLP and RVM Kurnool, Offices and Chief Planning Office, Kurnool for providing me information and data necessary for my research work.

I am also indebted to, Hyderabad, Centre for Economic and Social Studies, Hyderabad, Librarians and the staff of Libraries of Sri Krishnadevaraya University, Ananthapuramu who providing the necessary literature and data my topic.

I am also thankful to the respondents of School Dropout Children and Parents and officials whom I met during the course of my study, who were highly helpful to me in sparing their precious time in sharing their experiences.

I accolade my highest respect to my beloved parents **Smt.M.Govindamma** and **Sri.K.Seshi Reddy** and My Father-in-Law **Sri.P.Krishna Reddy** and My Mother- in –Law, **Smt.P.Kondamma** for their affectionnate love and blessings towards me and whose co-operation, moral support, constant encouragement and dedicated efforts to educate me to this level.

I must appreciate my husband **Sri.P.Anjaneya Reddy** for his encouragement and cooperation for successful completion of this academic task.

I express my thanks to my brother **M.V.Siva Reddy Superintendent (A.P.S.W.D.Kadapa)** and my sister-in-law **Smt.M.Maha Lakshmi** who feels my success as their success was behind me to come out successfully. I also record my sincere thanks to my well-wishers **Sri.V.V.L.Sekhar and Sri.K.Venkateswarlu** (Rtd. Superintendent, Social Welfare Department, Kurnool.), **G.Sudha Rani** Superintendent, Accounts Section, S.K.University for their encouragement to complete my research work.

I profusely thank my Co-Research Scholars K.Veera Nagendra, C.Eswaraiah, J.Madhusudan, G.Ramalingappa, G.Sankar Reddy who have extended their co-operation for the successful completion of my research work.

I record my thanks to all my friends particularly, L.Prathibha Chowdary, G.Radha, S.Bharathi, K.Radhika, and for their constant encouragement and moral support for the completion of my research thesis.

I express my thanks to Peeravali (Clerk), B.Akkulappa and Maruthi (Attenders) non-teaching staff in our Department. They are also more helpful co-operation for successful completion of my research work.

Last but not least my heart full thanks to Sri.P.Lokanna for his excellent computer work and help in successful completion of this work.

Finally, I thank and remember each and every person who helped me directly and indirectly in my career.

M. Sudha Parimala

CONTENTS

CHAPTER I
INTRODUCTION AND METHODOLOGY
INTRODUCTION

The most innocent phase in human life is the childhood. It is that stage of life when the human foundations are laid for a successful adult life. It is the phase when we are carefree, fun loving, learning, playing... A child is said to be the most beautiful creation of God. But not all children lead a happy life except those lucky ones who receive proper care and affection from their parents. There are children who had never enrolled in school. There are many children who drop out from school at a very early age. These children are deprived of basic education required for their socio-psychological development on sound lines, which would hamper their progress in the adulthood phase, thereby adversely affecting their meaningful participation in the development of a Nation. This is happening despite Constitutional provisions for compulsory education for all children in the age group of 6-14 years in India for over six decades.

The phenomenon of students discontinuing studies and repeating grades or completely dropping out from studies before completing elementary level of education is a major impediment in achieving the objective of Universalization of Elementary Education (UEE) in India. Besides, children never enrolled in school add to the problem. In order to assess the impact of this phenomenon on achievement of UEE, it is necessary to estimate dropout and repetition rates at primary and upper primary stages as well as transition rate from primary to upper primary level.

NATURE OF SCHOOL DROPOUT PROBLEM

The school dropout problem is a complex, multi-faceted problem, and the decision to drop out of school is a process, not an event. The contributing factors for this problem could be student-related, family-related, community-related, or school-related. While there are

1

many risk factors that indicate the potential to drop out, the presence of these factors or combinations of these factors do not necessarily mean that a student will drop out. The school dropout problem has been continually troubling the primary education system not only in India but also in other developing countries.

The dropout problem at school level is influenced by a series of independent factors namely school environment, prevalence of child labour, age of the child, negative attitude of parents towards education and the need to earn livelihood at an early stage of life among certain sections of children. Family migration and changes in residence are also responsible for dropout problem at school level.

DEFINITION OF SCHOOL DROPOUT

Under normal circumstances, school dropout indicates continuous absence of a child at the school. It is understood that any child who is absent to a class continuously for one month (30 days) for any reason could be considered as a dropout. It is important that the reasons like child ill-health, parental or child disinterest to attend the school for a period of more than 30 days need to be verified by the local teachers and corrective measures initiated to make the child attend the school regularly. If a child drops out of school due to reasons other than the above, that child is considered a dropout for the purpose of the present study. In operational terms, dropout rate refers to the percentage of pupils/ students who for any reason leave educational institutions during the school years (in any given grade or level) and did not come back to finish the grade or level during that school year to the total number of pupils/ students enrolled during the previous school year.

There are a number of ways through which retention and dropout rates are measured. Hundred minus retention rate is termed as gross dropout rate, which includes repeaters. Enrolment, attendance marked by the teachers and actual attendance of children in a class provide some basis to estimate the level of absenteeism of students in a school. If enrolment in a class during a specified year is less than the enrolment in a lower class in the preceding year, it indicates the school dropout problem. The reduction in the number of children would also have occurred due to transition. The following factors represent the different variants of children dropping out from school:

- When a child does not attend the school regularly and fail in a class at primary level because of lack of required attendance in an academic year.
- Within the above, the child would have been absent for the school as a result of health problems, temporary migration of family to other place or change of residence.
- When a child is entangled with subsidiary or family occupations, continuous absence to school may also occur.
- When a child takes Transfer Certificate and joins other school, it is presumed that the child is within the system, left the present school and joined the other school.
- Besides the above reasons, any child dropping out from school is considered voluntary and is described as Net dropout, because dropout due to the above factors can be addressed in one way or the other by designing a specific programme of action.

Absenteeism by children from schools, especially in a class, is characterized by non-retention, which includes Dropout also. Retention of children is as important as enrolment, because it indicates school effectiveness. But all the children in a class may not be promoted to subsequent higher class due to failure and lack of required attendance. The reasons listed above include both internal as well as external factors to the

3

system. Retention can be ensured by managing the internal factors and can be controlled by initiating action within the system.

IMPLICATIONS OF SCHOOL DROPOUT PROBLEM

Dropout of children from learning activities is a tremendous waste of child potential as it involves economic and social implications for future manpower development. Dropout from the school has the following effects:

1. Wastage of financial resources and child power, thereby affecting the socio-economic development of a nation.
2. It may give rise to and/ or intensify the problem of child labour.
3. Provision of quality education will be elusive.
4. Equity issues cannot be addressed.
5. Perpetual dropout problem makes it difficult to reach the goal of 100 per cent literacy at the national level.

RELATIONSHIP BETWEEN SCHOOL DROPOUT AND CHILD LABOUR PROBLEMS

The school dropout problem is primarily and directly related to the problem of child labour. Hence, it is important to address the problem of child labour in order to effectively tackle the school dropout problem. It is also true that effective tackling of school dropout problem results in eliminating the problem of child labour. Thus, an intricate relationship exists between these two problems. Not all the child labourers are school dropouts; there would be some children never enrolled in school. At the same time, not all the school dropouts are child labourers; there would be some children who sit at home. Nevertheless, it is true that most of the school dropouts are child labourers and vice versa.

As such, it becomes imperative to understand the different dimensions of child labour problem in order to evolve suitable policies/ measures for bringing the child labourers (out of school children including the school dropouts) into the mainstream of schooling system and thereby facilitating their meaningful participation in the development process.

THE PROBLEM OF CHILD LABOUR

The problem of Child Labour is a global phenomenon. Its magnitude and dimensions, however, vary widely from country to country. The obnoxious practice of child labour is widely prevalent in many of the developing countries such as India, China, Pakistan, Bangladesh, Nepal, Brazil, etc. Despite various measures undertaken by the government and the non-government agencies to tackle the exploitation of children, India acquired the dubious distinction of possessing a sizeable number of child labourers in the world.

From times immemorial, child labour has always existed under different names. Employment of children in different sectors of the economy is a fiat accompli of any and every Human Society, be it underdeveloped, developing or the developed one. While the problem is rampant in certain sectors and economies, it is less prevalent in other sectors. Nevertheless, the unorganized sector remains by far the most vulnerable sector where the magnitude of exploitation and abuse of children is found in an alarming proportion. The problem of child labour is widespread and is not a characteristic feature of any particular type of economy.

DEFINITION OF CHILD LABOUR

The term 'child labour' is used as a synonym for 'employed child' or 'working child'. It is very difficult to give a precise definition of child labour. Child labour could be defined as that segment of the child population which participates in work, either paid or unpaid. Any work by children that interferes with their full physical development, the opportunities for a desirable minimum of education and their needed recreation is called child labour (Stein and Davis, 1940). The All India Child

5

Labour Sample Survey commissioned by the Ministry of Labour in 1980-81 defined a working child as "that child who ... falling within the five to fifteen age brackets... is at enumerated work, may be paid or unpaid ... within or outside the family." Usually, the concept of child labour stands for the participation of children aged 14 years and below in the labour force for paid or unpaid work. Child labour is a widespread phenomenon. It is not only confined to work on family farm or in traditional family jobs and occupations but it has also extended to other fields. Child labour is found in agriculture and allied activities, unorg-anized small-scale sector and even in organized industries.

It is difficult to determine who falls under the category of 'child labourer' since it is culturally a relative term. According to the ILO Convention 138 - the standard setting instrument on child labour - the term refers to any child under a specifically defined age who is engaged in employment. The ILO considers the age group of 5-17 years for defining child labour. On the other hand, the government of India takes into account the child workers in the age group of 5-14 years as child labour. The definition of child labour as per the government of India norms is considered for the purpose of the present study.

In an effort to arrive at clear definitions of child labour, many academics, policy-makers, and others have begun to make a distinction between 'child work' and 'child labour'. Latin defines 'work' as any type of work being done in any mode of relationship. The concept of work serves as a description of the physical or mental involvement in the job. Labour, on the other hand, should be regarded as the production of goods and services that interferes with the normative development of children. This could also be the case when the child is doing strenuous household work that pre-empts schooling and leisure.

6

Many find the distinction between work and labour difficult to apply, since most of the work that children perform falls in the grey area in between these two extremes. White (1999) has developed a continuum that contains more gradations and that allows for more subtlety in assessing the nature of children's work. Rather than simply making a distinction between labour and work, the continuum makes distinction between work that is intolerable, detrimental or hazardous and work that is neutral or positive. The latter is the case, when, for example, work is not harmful, contributes to self-esteem and provides useful skills. On the basis of this continuum, children's engagement in activities that are considered intolerable, detrimental or hazardous should be considered as 'labour' and should generate concern and lead to intervention.

PERSISTENCE OF CHILD LABOUR

The problem of child labour continues to pose a challenge before the world. Governments have been taking various pro-active measures to tackle this problem. However, considering the magnitude and extent of the problem and that it is essentially a socio-economic problem inextricably linked to poverty and illiteracy, it requires concerted efforts from all sections of the society to make a dent in the problem.

Trends indicate that there has been a decline in the number of working children over time. The ILO estimates indicate that there were 78 million fewer child labourers in the age group of 5-17 years between 2000 and 2012 in the entire world, but even in 2012 the number of children in child labour stood at 168 million, accounting for 11 per cent of the child population as a whole. Of the total child labourers, those in the age group of 5-14 years accounted for 72 per cent.

In India, there were 1.26 crore working children in the age group of 5-14 years as compared to the total child population of 25.2 crore, accounting for 5 per cent of the total children according to 2001 Census. There were approximately 12 lakh children working in the hazardous occupations/ processes, which are covered under the Child Labour (Prohibition & Regulation) Act, 1986, i.e., 18 occupations and 65 processes. As per the survey conducted by National Sample Survey Organisation (NSSO) in 2004-05, the number of working children is estimated at 90.75 lakh. As per 2011 Census, the number of working children in the age group of 5-14 years declined to 43.53 lakh in the country. It shows that the efforts of the Government have yielded the desired fruits, but the problem still persists.

CRITICAL POLICY AREAS

Child labour is a stubborn problem that, even if overcome in certain places or sectors, will seek out opportunities to reappear in new and often unanticipated ways. The response to the problem must be as versatile and adaptable as child labour itself. There is no simple solution for child labour, nor a universal blueprint for action. Experience has shown that the effective elimination of child labour requires policies that address persistent poverty and the vulnerability of households to economic shocks Important policy responses concern education, social protection and efforts to promote decent work for adults.

STATEMENT OF THE PROBLEM

According to the Constitution of India, everyone has the fundamental right to be educated. Therefore, all sections of the population whether advantaged or disadvantaged, rich or poor, gifted or handicapped, rural or urban, male or female, Scheduled Tribe or Scheduled Caste, must be provided with educational opportunities. This is especially true in the case of the children since the Constitution has provided for compulsory education to all children in the age group of 6-14 years. Accordingly, the government initiated efforts to achieve universalization of elementary education.

8

But, a large number of children are discontinuing their education before completion of their schooling even in the present times. The large investments made by the government on education are being wasted. Several projects/ schemes have been implemented to arrest and reduce the dropout rate among the children in the age group of 6-14 years, but have not been effective in eliminating the 'school dropout problem'.

The government of India has implemented the National Child Labour Projects since 1988 with a focus on mainstreaming of school dropouts in the age group of 6-14 years through Residential Bridge Courses in all the districts with a high incidence of child labour. Despite such massive efforts, the school dropout problem still exists in some districts, which calls for in-depth investigations at the grassroots levels to analyse the reasons for this situation and to address the issue more effectively than before. Against this backdrop, the present study makes an attempt to examine the process of mainstreaming the school dropouts, to what extent this has been successful, what are the major impediments encountered, and how these can be overcome to realize the avowed aim of universalization of elementary education in the country.

REVIEW OF LITERATURE

Review of literature is the most important aspect in any research work. It is a measure stating the recent output on a particular area of research and organized in a helpful sequence to strengthen the present research techniques. The main objective of the review of literature is to understand the research activities that have taken place in a particular discipline in general and in the area of research in particular. A review of related literature on school dropout and child labour problems is presented here under.

Kundu (1984), reported that the problem of dropout among tribal students was because of inadequate attention to the development of tribal

9

language and culture, more stress on concessional provisions, education in non-tribal language, text books based on non-tribal literature and indifferent attitude of teachers towards tribal students.

Subramanyam (1986) studied the problem of dropout among Scheduled Tribe students in Andhra Pradesh. It was reported that the problem of dropout among scheduled tribe students was because the scheduled tribe students were unable to make adjustment with the present educational setup, inferiority complex among scheduled tribe students, mobility of the parents depending on their occupations from one place to another, tribal customs, traditions and negative attitude of parents towards girls' education.

Pal and Pant (1995) opined that since independence, universalization of elementary education has been an important public concern in India. A large number of programmes have been initiated by the Government to improve access to school education in the country. While these programmes have had a positive impact in some states and on some population groups, their overall impact is uneven and far from satisfactory. The differential performance of different states and population groups is a result of differential access to education. He further made an attempt to identify the relevant factors that could explain the inter-state variation in enrolment. Based on the relative importance of these factors, a strategy to improve access to education is outlined.

Reddy (1995) examined the factors determining the gross enrolment ratios of children at the primary and the upper primary/ middle levels of education, dropouts specially at the primary education level and the proportion of non-literate children in the age groups 6-11 and 6-14 years, with the help of Multiple Linear Regression Analysis for the rural and urban areas separately using the state level data collected by

10

National Sample Survey Organisation (NSSO) in its 42 round (July 1986 to June 1987) on "participation in education" in India. The important findings of this study are that even though the independent variables such as percentage of children in the age group 0-5 years, and literacy rate with primary and above education level (and also male as well as female literacy rates) among adults in the age group 15-44 years, have individually had significant association with the gross enrolment ratios of children at the primary and the upper primary/ middle levels and non-enrolment ratios of children in the age groups 6-11 and 6-14 years. In the case of rural areas, it was found that (i) the literacy rate with the primary and above education level among the male adults in the age group 15-44 years is the dominant explanatory variable for explaining the inter-state variations in the gross enrolment ratio of boys both at the primary and the upper primary levels and also of proportion of non-literate boys in the age groups 6-11 and 6-14 years; and (ii) the literacy rate with the primary and above education level among the female adults in the age group 15-44 years and the proportion of children in the age group 0-5 years are both needed to explain the inter-state variations in the gross enrolment ratio of girls at the primary level and also of proportion of non-literate girls in the age group of 6-14 years. In the case of urban areas, it was noted that the literacy rate with the primary and above education level among the female adults in the age group 15-44 years is the dominant explanatory variable found to be significant in explaining the gross enrolment ratios and proportion of non-literate children in the age groups 6-11 and 6-14 years. The regression results suggest that, other things remaining the same, an unit increase in literacy rate with the primary and above education level among the adults in the age group 15-44 years will result in about an unit decrease in the percentage of non-literate children in the age group of 6-11 years.

11

Ray (2000) used Indian unit record data from expenditure and employment surveys, in conjunction with state level indicators to (a) investigate whether the backward classes and female headed households face higher poverty rates than others; and (b) examine the impact of poverty, along with a host of individual, family, socio-economic and state characteristics, on child labour and child schooling. Special attention was paid to the gender issue and to the employment and schooling of children from the backward classes and female-headed households. The logit regression results point to the positive role that the state governments can play in improving child welfare.

Ray (2002) investigated into the key determinants of child labour hours and child schooling experience, paying special attention to the interaction between the two. A significant methodological feature that distinguished the study from previous investigations is that this analysis recognises the nexus among child labour, child schooling and child poverty. The study was conducted on Nepalese and Pakistani data. A key empirical finding, with significant policy implications, is the sharp trade-off between child labour and child schooling. Another common feature of both countries is the gender bias in favour of boys' schooling, though the bias is much larger in case of Pakistan.

Saxena (2004) opined that for educational advancement of tribals the Centre as well as the State Governments made hectic efforts to solve the problem of illiteracy and to educate tribals. The programmes such as Saksharta, Lok Jumbish, Adult Education, Non-Formal Education, Guru Mitra Yojna, etc., have been implemented in India but the results have defied expectations. In order to motivate the students to join the school and to continue the studies up to a particular stage, the government and other agencies arranged to give students free learning and instructional material, free mid-day meals, free uniform, scholarships, stipend, etc., but unfortunately as soon as these facilities were withdrawn, the students left the schools.

Mehta (2006) made an attempt with available data to discuss computation procedure of a variety of dropout and survival rates. He used the recent grade-specific enrolment and repeaters data of DISE to construct indicators of dropout. Broadly, the following methods have been discussed:

1. Average (Overall) Promotion, Repetition and Dropout Rate
2. Grade-to-Grade Transition Rate: Promotion, Repetition and Dropout Rate
3. Re-constructed Cohort Method: For calculating Cohort Dropout/Survival Rate and indicators of Internal Efficiency of Education system
4. Retention/Survival Rate
5. Transition from Primary to Upper Primary Level of Education.

Saravanan (2002) attempted to study the linkages between empowerment of women and reduction of child labour in the beedi industry in rural Tamil Nadu. The study analysed the socio-economic conditions of women and the nature and extent of child workers' participation in beedi making. It was argued that the initiatives taken to empower women in the beedi industry did not help reduce child labour, due to lacunae in the existing legal provisions and social security measures.

Jeyaranjan et al (2004) observed that Tamil Nadu's noon-cum-nutritious meal scheme is the country's largest in terms of the number of beneficiaries covered. There is little doubt that enrolment and retention of children, including girl children, in schools have shown significant improvement. In the two decades of the scheme's existence, the educational profile and the nature of problems at the ground level have changed significantly. If the midday meal is to retain its

13

effectiveness and relevance, it may have to be modified in the light of these changes.

Dev (2004) examined female work participation and child labour rates using occupational data from NFHS and compared this data with the 2001 Census and NSS data. Attempts were made to identify the determinants of both female work participation and child labour. It was found that the larger the size of the family, the lower is the ability of a woman to participate in economic activity.

Venkatanarayana (2004) stated that it is not convincing to accept that all out-of-school children are child labourers because, among other reasons, it sounds as if work and schooling are mutually exclusive activities for children. It was suggested that referring to them as educationally deprived children is justified from the perspective of human capital, development and human rights.

Balagopalan (2004) opined that the new draft bill on free and compulsory education justifies the parallel system of schooling by juxtaposing the moral urgency of schooling as 'opportunity' versus unbridled toil of the child labourer. The two-tier system of schools contradicts its own high-minded endeavour of having schooling serve as a means to end child labour. Schooling becomes compulsory for fear of drawing penalty, while little attention is paid to ensuring quality education.

Bill and Melinda Foundation (2006) noted that there is a high school dropout epidemic in America. It approached the dropout problem from a perspective that has not been much considered in past studies - that of the students themselves. The report revealed that each year, almost one-third of all public high school students - and nearly one half of all blacks, Hispanics and Native Americans - fail to graduate from public high school with their class. Many of these students abandoned school with less than two years to complete their high school education.

Grant and Hallman (2006) examined the factors associated with schoolgirl pregnancy, as well as the likelihood of school dropout and subsequent re-enrolment among pregnant schoolgirls in KwaZulu-Natal province of South Africa. Their analysis triangulates data collected from birth histories, education histories, and data concerning pregnancy to strengthen the identification of young women who became pregnant while enrolled in school and to define discrete periods of school interruption prior to first pregnancy. They found that prior school performance - defined as instances of grade repetition or non-pregnancy related temporary withdrawals from school - is strongly associated with a young woman's likelihood of becoming pregnant while enrolled in school, dropping out of school if she becomes pregnant, and not returning to school following a pregnancy-related dropout. Young women who were the primary caregivers to their children are also significantly more likely to have left school than are women who shared or relinquished childcare responsibilities. Furthermore, young women who lived with an adult female were significantly more likely to return to school following a pregnancy-related dropout. Given the increasing levels of female school participation in sub-Saharan Africa, their findings suggest that future studies will benefit from exploring the causal relationships between prior school experiences, adolescent reproductive behaviour, and subsequent school attendance.

Alliance for Excellent Education (2007) made an assessment of the problem of high school dropouts in USA. The study revealed that each dropout, over his or her lifetime, costs the nation approximately $260,000. Most high school dropouts see the result of their decision to leave school most clearly in the slimness of their wallets. It estimated that the average annual

15

income for a high school dropout in 2005 was $17,299, compared to $26,933 for a high school graduate, a difference of $9,634 (U.S. Bureau of the Census, 2006). The impact on the country's economy is less visible, but it is nevertheless staggering.

Choudhury (2006) noted that while progress in improving literacy in India has been remarkable, the phenomenon of school dropouts has remained a blot in the face of an otherwise commendable performance. Dropout rates undoubtedly came down but were still high. Sex differentials also reduced. But rates for females consistently remained above those of males.

Peter et al (2007) attempted at culling out the factors involved in making students from the Scheduled Caste (SC) and Scheduled Tribe (ST) categories to drop out of school. The study found that most of them attend school to have the noon meal and avail monetary benefits like waiver on exam fees, free uniforms and books. As soon as they join secondary school, scheduled caste / scheduled tribe students find it difficult to start their own business and get employment only in unskilled jobs. It was concluded that the scheduled caste and scheduled tribe students of the corporation schools are compelled to leave the school abruptly because of multifarious reasons, but predominantly for economic compulsions and social causes.

Usha (2007) finds fault with the estimation of dropout rate. The dropout rate estimated from official statistics is calculated as the ratio of enrolment in (say) class V to enrolment in class I. Such an estimate of dropout rates could be misleading given that official enrolment statistics are known to be highly unreliable. Further, there is some evidence that class I enrolment is often inflated, and this has the effect of magnifying the dropout rate estimates based on official enrolment data.

Das (2007) made a study of Sarva Siksha Abhiyan and found a promising reduction in dropout rates especially for girls; however, the quality of

16

infrastructure and teaching standards in government schools leaves much to be desired.

Kumar and Latika (2008) observed that addressing gender disparity in education goes beyond increasing the presence of girls in school. It involves the removal of deep mental blocks that bind them to limited traditional roles. Based on the functioning of the Kasturba Gandhi Balika Vidyalaya, the study highlights the problems impeding girls' overall development. If the KGBV is to be given a second chance for mainstreaming rural girls belonging to deprived social backgrounds, it needs to set right certain shortcomings.

Bhattacharya (2008) attempted to predict the percentage of districts with school dropout rate of less than 10per cent at primary level (grades one through five) in the eastern region of India. It was found that there is a strong statistical evidence (p-value=0.9928) for the use of Beta - Binomial model as an effective tool for assessing the school dropout rate. It was estimated that in the next three years, only 25per cent of the districts in eastern region are expected to achieve the targeted dropout rate of less than 10per cent, whereas 20per cent of the districts are expected to have more than 10per cent dropout rate.

Venkatanarayana (2009) pointed out that it is not the dropout rate, but rather the high rate of non-enrolment, which is the real reason for education deprivation. If the goal of universalization of elementary education is to be achieved there is a strong need for an enrolment drive and an action plan to ensure the attendance and retention of those enrolled.

Guha and Sengupta (2002) studied the impact of household demand factors on the school participation and performance in four villages and two urban wards of West Bengal. The aim of the study was to assess the relative importance of these factors on the schooling choices made for girl children. The results indicated that some of the strongest enabling factors with regard to girls' school participation and grade attainment were household resource factors such as parental, especially maternal schooling, father's occupation, and family income. Urban residence, as expected, had a strong positive association, and significant cohort effects were observed with regard to the schooling outcomes. A girl child's labour force participation significantly reduced the demand for schooling, and the amount of schooling obtained. Religion and caste factors emerged as important determinants of schooling, as well.

Mario et al (2009) observed that child labour is widespread in home-based manufacturing activities in the informal sector in most developing countries. However, very little is known of child labour in industrial outwork.

Govindaraju and Venkatesan (2010) carried out a cross sectional survey of school dropouts in rural settings by using open-ended interview formats and demographic data sheet on a sample of 120 parents, teachers and dropout children. They reported nearly 60 reasons for school dropout. Their empirical domain-wise classification revealed three major clusters with significant differences in the reported causes in relation to gender, occupation and educational status of teachers: school education status, education of parents and gender of the dropout children. The results were presented and implications for their remediation discussed illustratively on a triple Venn diagram with intersecting subsets of overlapping and independent perceptions between the respondents-parents, teachers and dropout students respectively.

Reddy and Sinha (2010) attempted to assess the magnitude of the problem of dropout. They critically reviewed the evidence on some of the commonly cited reasons for dropout, including poverty, limited access to credit, child labour, and children's and parents' lack of interest in education. They argued that the literature rarely looks at the role of procedures and rules in schools and the wider education system in terms of pushing children out of school. They contended that the reason for persistently high dropout rate should be located in the absence of a social norm in terms of children's right to education; and that this is reflected in the lack of systemic support available for children at risk of dropping out. The paper also documented an experiment initiated by MV Foundation in Shankarpalle Mandal, Ranga Reddy district, Andhra Pradesh, where procedures, rules and practices relating to various aspects of school were changed to ensure that every child stayed in school and completed elementary level.

Kumar (2011) appraised the efforts of Karnataka state government and civil society in rescuing and rehabilitating child labourers in the state. The author argued that the mainstreaming is the ultimate goal of the entire attempt to eradicate child labour.

Dev and George (2012) attempted to distinguish between eliminating and ending child labour from production networks as the former deals with the demand-side while the latter deals with the supply-side of the child labour equation. They concluded that while corporate initiatives could deal with the demand-side, government development and social policy intervention is required to deal with the supply-side.

Basumatary (2012) opined that that the school dropout depends upon various factors such as poverty level, distance of school from home, transport facilities, quality of teachers, social environment and many other factors. The study made a quantitative analysis of school dropout rate, which is regressed on various variables referred to as factors. The data for school dropout rates and many other variables across Indian states and UTs are considered for the session 2009-10. The study found statistically significant impact of state poverty level and the rural population on school dropout.

Sikdar and Mukhejee (2012) found that improving quality and mitigating financial constraints, especially for the lower classes, could achieve universal enrolment, retention and completion in both elementary and secondary education.

Nithiya and Kundupuzhakkal (2013) examined the dropout rate of children from primary to secondary level. It was found that the number of dropouts is high in all the periods at secondary level. It was concluded that the mind-set of the society towards gender-based discrimination should be changed with the help of Educators, Administrators, and Policymakers.

Joy and Srihari (2014) enquired into the hidden reasons for the increasing school dropouts among the ST students of Wayanad district, with special reference to the Paniya Tribe. The study analysed 2007-12 academic year dropout rates in detail from the tribal populated district of Wayanad. It was found that the major reason for the increased dropout rate is the lack of awareness on the value of education among the scheduled tribes. Qualitative analysis and case studies were used to elicit the reasons for the increase of tribal dropout rate in the district. The findings of the study provided adequate solutions for the high dropout rate among tribals in the form of implementing strong constructivist pedagogy and class-oriented learning approach in the tribal areas.

RESEARCH GAP AND NEED FOR THE STUDY

Studies pointed out differential access to education or uneven distribution of education across different spatial and socio-economic groups as the main reason for the varied performance of different states in achieving universalization of elementary education. Empirical evidence indicated a sharp trade-off between child labour and child schooling and gender bias in favour of boys' schooling. Some studies made efforts to determine the factors responsible for the school dropout problem in different contexts. Some studies focussed on factors motivating the students to remain in school. Some other studies attempted to identify the shortcomings or constraints in implementation of different schemes aimed at reducing the dropout rate among school children by increasing the enrolment and retention rates. A few other studies addressed the issues of divergence relating to construction of indicators for dropout and methods of estimating the dropout rate.

Most of the studies were based on secondary data and attempted to bring out the relationship between school dropout problem and other factors such as poverty, literacy rate, educational status and absence of schooling facilities at the macro level. Not many studies were conducted at the grassroots level, focussing on the factors responsible for the persistence of child labour and school dropout problems and on identifying the constraints in the implementation mechanism, besides the rules and procedures governing the implementation of different schemes for achieving universalization of elementary education. Considering the widespread prevalence of the problem and large-scale variations in socio-economic and physical characteristics, the number of studies conducted across different states and socio-economic groups could be considered as scarce. Further, comprehensive studies analysing the problem from the point of view of children who dropped out from school, parents of school dropouts, schooling system and implementation mechanism of specific projects/ schemes aimed at mainstreaming the school dropouts are rather limited. Very few studies were conducted at grassroots level in Andhra Pradesh, especially in drought prone and backward regions like Rayalaseema. In this context the present study is a modest attempt to examine the issues and problems in mainstreaming the school dropouts in a backward district of Rayalaseema region in Andhra Pradesh.

21

OPERATIONAL DEFINITION OF TERMS USED IN THE STUDY

The operational definition of the important terms used in the study is given below:

Dropout rate: Refers to the percentage of pupils/students who for any reason leave educational institutions during the school years (in any given grade or level) and did not come back to finish the grade or level during that school year to the total number of pupils/students enrolled during the previous school year.

Gross enrollment Ratio: Refers to the total enrolment of students in a grade or level of education, regardless of age, expressed as percentage of the corresponding eligible official age group population in a given school year.

Net enrollment Ratio: Refers to the number of students enrolled in the official specific age group expressed as a percentage of the total population in that age group.

Repetition Rate: Percentage of pupils/students who enroll in the same grade/year more than once to the number of pupils/ students enrolled in that grade/year during the previous year.

Transition Rate: Percentage of students who graduated from one level of education, e.g, primary, secondary, etc., and moved on or enroll to the next higher level.

Completion rate: The percentage of pupils/students enrolled at the beginning grade/year of the level of education who finished or graduated from the final grade/year at the end of the required number of years of that level of education.

Education system: Refers to the entirely organized and sustained process of providing education to groups of people regardless of age according to their learning needs. The activities, structure and hierarchy may differ from one setting to another. The process of delivery to the learners comes in such basic forms as formal and non-formal by either a public/government entity or a private organization.

OBJECTIVES OF THE STUDY

The study aimed to examine whether the interventions made in mainstreaming the school dropouts were successful and whether the process resulted in eliminating the school dropout problem, in the context of Kurnool district of Andhra Pradesh, where the intensity of the problem was high. The specific objectives of the study are:

1. To study the school dropout problem in all its dimensions in Andhra Pradesh with special reference to Kurnool district;

2. To understand the socio-economic charac-teristics of the school dropouts and their households, and to ascertain the causes for their dropping out from school in the study area;

3. To examine the role of government agencies and NGOs in mainstreaming the school dropouts in the study area;

4. To identify the constraints in the implementation of National Child Labour Project and Sarva Siksha Abhiyan programme in the study area; and

5. To suggest measures, in the light of the findings of the study, for effectively mainstreaming the school dropouts and to eliminate the menacing problem of child labour.

METHODOLOGY

The methodological aspects of the study such as the area of the study, the universe and the sample, sources of data, tools of data collection, analysis of data, chapter scheme, limitations and significance of the study are detailed here under.

AREA OF THE STUDY

Being a study undertaken by an individual researcher, it was decided to confine the study to one district in Andhra Pradesh. Kurnool district, which had

23

the highest number of out-of-school children (school dropouts and never enrolled children) in Rayalaseema region, was specifically chosen for the purpose of the study.

THE UNIVERSE AND THE SAMPLE

All the out-of-school children who were enrolled in residential bridge courses (RBCs) in Kurnool district during 2007-08 and 2008-09 constitute the universe of the study. The RBCs were started as part of National Child Labour Project (NCLP) with the objective of mainstreaming the out-of-school children including school dropouts by giving them adequate orientation and ensuring their admission into formal education system (government residential and non-residential schools). Since the study was period under consideration of the 2009-10, the enrolment in RBCs during the immediate two preceding years was taken as the criterion for determining the universe, because there is not much lapse between the enrolment in RBCs and admission into government schools and the recall regarding the process would not be a problem.

A combination of Multi-stage, purposive and random sampling methods was used to select the sample for the study. At the first stage, it was decided to give representation to all the revenue divisions in Kurnool district. The district had three revenue divisions, viz., Kurnool, Adoni and Nandyal, comprising a total of 54 revenue Mandals. At the second stage, it was decided to choose one mandal from each revenue division on the basis of highest enrolment in RBCs during the period under consideration under consideration (2007-08 to 2008-09). The details of out-of-school children enrolled in RBCs during the period under consideration were collected for the selected three mandals. At the third stage, 2-3 villages were chosen from each selected mandal, again based on the highest enrolment in RBCs during the period under consideration. At the last stage, it was decided to choose a sample of 80 out-of-school children enrolled in RBCs during the reference from the sample villages on the basis of random sampling method. Thus, the study covers a sample of 240 out-of-school children (mostly school dropouts) enrolled in RBCs during the period under consideration (2007-08 and 2008-09) from 8 villages falling under 3 mandals of all the three revenue divisions in Kurnool district. The sampling framework of the study is presented in table 1.1

Table – 1.1
Sampling Framework of the Study

Name of the Revenue Division	Name of the Mandal	Name of the Village	No. of Respondents
Adoni	Peddakadabur	1. Peddakadabur	20
		2. Gavigattu	60
Nandyal	Allagadda	1. Allagadda	30
		2. Obulampalli	30
		3. Ahobilam	20
Kurnool	Kallur	1. Lakshmipuram	30
		2. Chinna Tekur	20
		3. Weavers Colony	30
Total		8	240

Sources of data and tools of data collection

To examine the objectives of this study, relevant data were collected from both primary and secondary sources. Field Survey was undertaken for collection of primary data. The Field Survey was conducted in 2009. For this purpose, a pre-tested interview schedule was employed to collect the primary data from the school dropouts and also from their parents. Further, observation technique was followed to understand certain aspects of the problem. The data collected from the sample respondents relating to the causes and consequences of dropout from school in Kurnool district were thoroughly analysed.

Besides, secondary data regarding educational scenario and schemes in India and in Andhra Pradesh and data regarding enrolment and dropout rate in Kurnool district were collected from different published and unpublished records, which include Reports of the Department of Education, Ministry of Human Resource Development, Government of India, Reports of the Directorate of Education, Government of Andhra Pradesh, Reports of Office the Sarva Siksha Abhayan, Kurnool and records of District Educational Office, Kurnool district, Statistical Abstracts of Government of Andhra Pradesh and Kurnool District, etc.

Analysis of data and use of statistical tools

The collected data were processed and analysed both manually and with the help of a computer. Both primary and secondary data were tabulated to bring out systematic analysis of the school dropout rate and mainstreaming efforts to reduce the dropout rate. Statistical tools like averages and percentages were used for interpretation of data.

CHAPTER SCHEME

The results of the study are presented in six chapters as detailed below:

Chapter-I : **Introduction and Methodology**
It contains a brief introduction to the problem and conceptual framework of the study.

Chapter-II : **Child Labour and School Dropout problems in India: An Overview**
It presents the scenario of child labour and school dropout problems at the National level, causes for school dropout problem, and the projects/ schemes implemented to mainstream the school dropouts and the results achieved in eliminating the problem of child labour.

Chapter-III : **Mainstreaming of School Dropouts in A.P with Special Reference to Kurnool**

District

It discusses various schemes introduced by the Government to increase the enrolment rate and reduce the dropout rate and their implications at State and District level. It also presents the process of mainstreaming the school dropouts under NCLP and SSA in Kurnool district, including the identification of out-of-school children, assess the reasons for being out of school, strategies formulated to enrol them into bridge courses and other alternative and innovative education centres, achievements made and the impact of such process at the district level.

Chapter-IV : **Socio-Economic profile of Sample Children and Households**

It presents the socio-economic profile of sample children and their households, which have a bearing on the school dropout problem and also on the process of mainstreaming the sample children into formal education system.

Chapter-V : **Mainstreaming of School Dropouts in the Study Area: An Empirical Analysis**

It analyses the perceptions of respondents on various facets of school dropout problem and their mainstreaming into formal education system, and the interventions made by the government, results achieved and constraints identified.

Chapter-VI : **Summary and Conclusions**

It summarises the major findings of the study and draws conclusions and discusses the policy implications.

LIMITATIONS OF THE STUDY

The study was confined to only one district in Rayalaseema region of Andhra Pradesh, and hence, the results cannot be generalized at the state or national level. The primary data was collected from the school dropouts and their parents by using recall method, and the data may not be precise, despite efforts made to probe into the details. The secondary data collected from various published and unpublished sources may not be accurate, given the deficiencies in the methods of collecting and compiling the data and the loopholes in the administrative system. These limitations may be borne in mind while analysing the results of the study.

SIGNIFICANCE OF THE STUDY

In spite of the above limitations, the study assumes significance as it is based on primary data and attempts to capture the perspectives of school dropouts and their parents on the school dropout and child labour problems. The study also assumes significance as it focuses on examining the implementation of National Child Labour Project insofar it is concerned with mainstreaming the school dropouts at the grassroots level and attempts to identify the constraints in the implementation process. The study is also important as it makes judicious use of information collected from different sources and attempts to examine the success of interventions to tackle the school dropout problem, which may throw light on measures needed for eliminating the problem of child labour. Besides, the study is an attempt to fill the research gap in the field to some extent.

References

Alliance for Excellent Education, (2007) "The High Cost of High School Dropouts What the Nation Pays for Inadequate High Schools" www. all4ed.org.

Amarendra Das, (2007), "How Far Have We Come in Sarva Siksha Abhayan", *Economic and Political Weekly*, Vol – XLII No. 01, January.

Anil Kumar.V (2011), "State, Civil Society and the Eradication of Child Labour in Karnataka", *Economic and Political Weekly* ,Vol – XLVI No. 03 January 15, 2011.

Anugula N. Reddy and Shanta Sinha, (2010), "School Dropouts or Pushouts? Overcoming Barriers for the Right to Education", National University of Educational Planning and Administration, Research Monograph No. 40, July.

Basumatary, (2012), "School Dropout across Indian States and UTs: An Econometric Study", *International Research Journal of Social Sciences*,Vol. 1(4), 28-35, December, pp.28-35.

Bhattacharya Abhijit "Assessing School Drop-out Rate at Primary Level in Eastern Region of India" *Advances in Management*, Vol. 1, No.3, September, 2008, pp. 5-8.

Bill and Melinda Foundation, (2006), "The Silent Epidemic: perspective of High School Dropouts".

Choudary, (2006) "Special Article", *Economic and Political Weekly*, VOl – XLI No. 51, December 23.

Dev Nathan and Ann George, (2012), "Corporate Governance and Child Labour" *Economic and Political Weekly*, Vol. - XLVII No. 50, December 15.

Dev S. (2004), "Female Work Participation and Child Labour" Economic and Political Weekly, Vol. XXXIX No. 07, February 14.

Govindaraju.R and Venkatesan.S (2010), "A Study on School Drop-outs in Rural Settings" *Journal of Psychology*, Vol. 1, No.1, pp.47-53.

Jaba Guha and Piyali Sengupta (2002), "Enrollment, Dropout and Grade Completion of Girl Children in West Bengal", Review of Women's Studies Review Issues Specials, *Economic and Political Weekly*, Vol - XXXVII No. 17, April.

Jeyaranjan J (2004), "Women Studies Review Issues Specials", Economic and Political Weekly , Vl – XXXIX No.44, October 30.

Jobin Joy and M. Srihari, (2014), "A Case study on the School dropout Scheduled Tribal students of

Wayanad District, Kerala", *Research Journal of Educational Sciences*, Vol. 2(3), 1-6,June, pp.1-6.

Krishna Kumar and Latika Gupta, "What Is Missing in Girls' Empowerment", *Economic and Political Weekl* ,Vol – XLIII No. 26-27, June 28, 2008.

Kukreti Manoj Kumar Saxena B.R, (2004), "Dropout Problem among Tribal /Students at School Level: A Case Study," Kurukshetra, Vol.52, No.11, September.

Kundu, (1984), "Tribal Education in India: Some Problems", Journal of Indian Education 10(2), pp.1-7.

Mario Biggeri, Ratna M Sudharshan and Santosh Mehrotra (2009), "Child Labour in Industrial Outworker Households in India" *Economic and Political Weekly,* Vol – XLIV No.12, March 21

Mehta C, (2006) "Drop-out Rate at Primary Level: A Note based on DISE 2003- 04 & 2004-05 Data " National Institute of Educational Planning and administration, New Delhi.

Monica and Kelly Hallman, (2006), "Pregnancy-related Dropout and Prior School Performance in South Africa", Working Paper No.212, Population Council, New York.

Nithiya Amirtham S and Saidalavi Kundupuzhakkal, (2013), "Gender Issues and Dropout Rates in India: Major Barrier in Providing Education for All", *Educationia Confab,* Vol. 2, No. 4, April , pp.226-233.

Pal S.P and D.K. Pant (1995), "Strategies to improve School Enrollment" Journal of Educational Planning and Administration Vol. IX, No. 2, April 1995. pp. 159-168.

Peter.S, Raman K.J and Ravilochanan.P (2006), "School Dropouts of SC and ST Students in Chennai Corporation Schools", The Indian Journal of Social Work, Vol.68, Issue 2, April 2007, pp.248-258.

Ranjan Ray (2000), Poverty, Household Size and Child Welfare in India, Economic and Political Weekly, Vol. XXXV No. 39, September 23.

Ranjan Ray (2002), "Simultaneous Analysis of Child Labour and Child Schooling", Economic and Political Weekly, Vol.XXXVII No. 52, December 28, 2002.

Reddy V.N (1995), "Gross Enrolment, Drop-Out and Non-Enrolment Ratios in India: A State Level Analysis", Journal of Educational Planning and Administration, Vol. IX, No.3, July. pp. 229-254.

Sarada Balagopalan, (2004), "Free and Compulsory Education Bill, 2004", *Economic and Political Weekly* , Vol – XXXIX No. 32, August 07, 2004.

Saravanan, (2002) "Women's Employment and Reduction of Child Labour", Economic and Political Weekly, Vol. XXXVII No. 52,December 28.

Satadru Sikdar (2012), and Anit N Mukherjee, "Enrolment and Dropout Rate in School Education", *Economic and Political Weekly*,Vol – XLVII No.01, January 07.

Subrahmanyam (1986), "Problems of School Dropouts: A Study with Special Reference to SC and ST in Andhra Pradesh", Education Quarterly, 38(3), pp.28-32.

Usha (2007), "How High are Drop-out Rates in India?", Economic and Political Weekly March 17, p.982.

Venkata Narayana.M (2009), "Out of school children: Child labourers or educationally deprived" , *Economic and Political Weekly*, vol 39, No 38 p 4219.

Venkatanarayana. M (2004), "Out-of-School Children", *Economic and Political Weekly* , Vol,XXXIX No.38, September.

CHAPTER-II
CHILD LABOUR AND SCHOOL DROPOUT PROBLEMS
IN INDIA: AN OVERVIEW
INTRODUCTION

The school dropout problem is pervasive in the Indian education system. Many children, who enter school, are unable to complete secondary education. Multiple factors are responsible for children dropping out of school. Risk factors begin to add up even before students enrol in school; these include poverty, low educational level of parents, weak family structure, pattern of schooling of siblings, and lack of pre-school experiences. Family background and domestic problems create an environment, which negatively affects the value of education. Further, students could drop out as a result of a multitude of school factors such as uncongenial atmosphere, poor comprehension, absenteeism, attitude and behaviour of the teachers, and failure or repetition in the same grade, etc. When students experience school failure, they become frustrated with lack of achievement and end up alienated and experience exclusion, leading to eventual dropout. It is important to carefully design preventive measures and intervention strategies that could be adopted in order to help all school dropouts. Certain preventive measures can be implemented throughout the target population, while others must take into account the diversity of dropout profiles. In this chapter, an attempt is made to study the problems of child labour and school dropout and their inter-relationship. An overview of the different dimensions of child labour, attempts to eliminate child labour, progress made under the National Child Labour Project (NCLP), the school dropout scenario and the measures needed to address the residual and equity gaps in elementary education at the national level is provided in this chapter.

CHILD LABOUR AND EDUCATION

Studies on the universalization of primary education tended to neglect the problem of child labour. Research in the field of child labour mostly focused on the deleterious effects it has on children's health and growth as well as the exploitative conditions of work. These two subject areas have been compartmentalized and separated from each other in the organization of government departments as also in the operations of international agencies.

Three categories of children engaged in work could be distinguished: child labour, working children and street children. Child labour has usually been defined to refer to children who work for those other than their families and normally for a wage; working children are taken to mean those who work as part of family labour; and street children are those who work in semi-urban and urban centres and live either in their employers' premises or, literally, on the streets. These distinctions, useful for analytical purposes, are not always replicated in reality and there is frequent overlap amongst the categories. Different countries define child labour in different ways with differing criteria of age, and it is therefore important to consider the available statistics in the light of the definitions employed. In one sense, a quest for precision in numbers is futile; in another sense, one must be alive to attempt to underestimate the magnitude of the problem.

About 90 per cent of India's working children live in the rural areas and are usually involved with some kind of agricultural or allied activity. Boys and girls in village India take some of the burden from their parents in jobs like tending cattle, fetching water, fuel and fodder, cooking, cleaning and other domestic chores. Girl children tend to concentrate on domestic activity but as a result of the contribution of children, parents are able to go out and earn a living. As children grow older, they become more directly involved with

33

agricultural operations like sowing, weeding, transplanting, harvesting and so on. During seasonal operations, such children are unable to attend school even if their parents wished them to and could afford to send them.

The Indian school system has a single point entry and consists of a sequential and full-time format of institutional instruction by full-time and professional teachers. Naik (1975) argued for a radical transformation in the traditional model of formal education. Despite the advantages of the single point entry method, such as the creation of a homogeneous age group cohort, which rises year after year to successively higher classes, it means that the child who is unable to enter school at class 1 at the age of six remains outside it forever. Although in principle the same child could enter class 1 at age 11, he would have to be with much younger children and despite his readiness to go faster, he would have to learn at the same speed.

There is a point of view frequently propounded by professionals in the field of education and policy makers that the existing school system is irrelevant to the needs of working children. It is argued that sterile curricula, rote-based learning and the poor quality of teachers, amongst other ills, plague the school system and that, therefore, neither the parents of working children nor the children themselves are keen to gain access to it. To argue that the parents of working children do not send them to school primarily because of the supposed irrelevance of the curricula is profoundly mistaken. Rather, evidence from the field suggests that parents have a deep interest in educating their children for the mobility that education alone can provide to the socially and economically disadvantaged sections of society. Commonly, difficult economic circumstances prevent the fulfilment of this aspiration;

inadequate school infrastructure tilts the balance in favour of work.

DISTRIBUTION OF CHILD WORKING POPULATION: CENSUS DATA

The distribution of Child labour across the states in India from 1971 to 2011 is shown in table 2.1.

Table 2.1

State-wise Child Labour in India from 1971 to 2011: Census Data

S. No	Name of the State/UT	1971	1981	1991	2001	2011
1	Andhra Pradesh	1627492	1951312	1661940	1363339	404851
2	Assam*	239349	**	327598	351416	99512
3	Bihar	1059359	1101764	942245	111700	451590
4	Gujarat	518061	616913	523585	485530	250318
5	Haryana	137826	194189	109691	253491	53492
6	Himachal Pradesh	71384	99624	56438	107774	15001
7	Jammu& Kashmir	70489	258437	**	175630	25528
8	Karnataka	808719	1131530	976247	822615	249432
9	Kerala	111801	92854	34800	26156	21757
10	Madhya Pradesh	1112319	1698597	1352563	1065259	286310
11	Maharashtra	988357	1557756	1068427	764075	496916
12	Chhattisgarh	-	-	-	364572	63884
13	Manipur	16380	20217	16493	28836	11805
14	Meghalaya	30440	44916	34633	53940	18839
15	Jharkhand	-	-	-	407200	90996
16	Uttarakhand	-	-	-	70183	28098
17	Nagaland	13726	16235	16467	45874	11062
18	Odisha	492477	702293	452394	377594	92087
19	Punjab	232774	216939	142868	1772688	90353
20	Rajasthan	587389	819605	774199	1262570	252338
21	Sikkim	15661	8561	5598	16457	2704
22	Tamil Nadu	713305	975055	578889	418801	151437
23	Tripura	17490	24204	16478	21756	4998
24	Uttar Pradesh	1326726	1434675	1410086	1927997	896301
25	West Bengal	511443	605263	711691	857087	234275

26	Andaman& Nicobar Islands	572	1309	12565	1960	999
27	Arunachal Pradesh	17925	17950	12395	18482	5766
28	Chandigarh	1086	1986	1870	3779	3135
29	Dadra & Nagar Haveli	3102	3615	4416	4274	1054
30	Delhi	17120	25717	27351	41899	26473
31	Daman &Diu	7391	9378	941	729	774
32	Goa	-	-	4656	4138	6920
33	Lakshadweep	97	56	34	27	28
34	Mizoram		6314	16411	26265	2793
35	Pondicherry	3725	3606	2680	1904	1421
	Total	**10753985**	**13640870**	**11285349**	**12666377**	**4353247**

Source: Census Reports-1971 to 2011: Registrar General, Census of India.

As per the 1971 Census in India, it was found that child working population comprised 10,753,985 persons engaged in different jobs and that 15.13 **per cent** of child labour was engaged in Andhra Pradesh **alone,** which was the highest child labour affected state of India. On the other hand, Lakshadweep, with a child working population of 97 persons in 1971, was the lowest child labour affected state in India. The trends in child labour growth in 1981 and 1991 were similar to that of 1971 Census. The situation changed with regard to the place of Andhra Pradesh in child labour in 2001 and 2011, when Uttar Pradesh accounted for the highest number of child labour in India, accounting for 15.22 per cent and 20.59 per cent of total child labour in the country, respectively.

DIFFERENT DIMENSIONS OF CHILD WORKERS: NSSO DATA, 2009-10

The 66th Round of Survey on Employment and Unemployment (2009-10) conducted by the NSSO provides the data on different dimensions of the child workers (5-14 years) in India. An attempt is made here to analyse the basic characteristics and different dimensions of child workers.

Profile of child workers

Table 2.2 shows the profile of child labour by place of residence and sex, from which it becomes evident that the problem of child labour is more prevalent in rural areas than in urban. It could be noted that the median age of the child labour was 13 years. The proportion of child labour in total workforce of the country stood at 1.09 per cent, being highest in respect of rural females (1.53 per cent) and lowest in the case of urban males (0.53 per cent). Proportion in work force is the per cent of children aged (5-14) of the total work force of the country. The proportion of illiterates among the child labourers stood at 28 per cent in the country, without much variation across the gender and place of residence. Both the Child Work Participation Rate (children employed per 1000 children) and the Child Labour Force Participation (children employed as well as seeking any kind of employment per 1000 children) stood at 20, being highest in rural males and lowest in urban females.

Table 2.2
Profile of Child Labour: NSSO Survey, 2009-10

Particulars	Rural		Urban		Total All India
	Male	Female	Male	Female	
Median Age of Child Labour	13	13	13	13	13
Proportion of Illiterate child labourers (%)	26.04	29.93	29.87	27.27	27.84
Proportion in workforce (%)	1.07	1.65	0.53	0.85	1.09
Child WPR (per 1000)	24	20	15	7	20
Child LFPR (per 1000)	26	20	16	7	20

Source: Unit Level Records of NSSO

STATE-WISE DISTRIBUTION OF CHILD WORKERS

The distribution of children in workforce by states/ union territories in India in two age groups, 5-9 years and 10-14 years by place of residence and sex is shown in table 2.3. It could be seen that most of the child workers were concentrated in rural areas in the age group of 10-14 years. Among the child workers, 51 per cent were rural males and 36 per cent rural females. The child workers in the age group of 5-9 years accounted for about 8 per cent of total and pose a serious threat to the nation. Uttar Pradesh accounted for highest percentage of child workers (35%). Andhra Pradesh stood at 7th position in the country in terms of percentage of child workers (4.78%). On the other hand, the union territories and the north-eastern states show impressive figures on child labour. It is paradoxical to note that the states with high GDP share in the nation also have high incidence of child labour. This necessitates re-examination of the question on the ability of GDP to achieve human development along with economic development.

Table2.3
State-wise Distribution of Children in Workforce:
NSSO Survey, 2009-10

Name of the State / U.T.	Rural				Urban				State share
	Male		Female		Male		Female		
	Age (5-9)	Age (10-14)	Age (5-9)	Age (10-14)	Age (5-9)	Age (10-14)	Age (5-9)	Age (10-14)	
Uttar Pradesh	1.27	18.6	1.92	9.14	0.21	2.53	0.13	1.19	34.98
West Bengal	0.29	7.02	0	2.6	0	0.52	0.01	0.46	10.9
Rajasthan	0.38	1.57	0.64	4.93	0	0.89	0	0.17	8.58
Gujarat	0.8	2.4	0.61	3.67	0	0.31	0	0.33	8.13
Bihar	0.36	4.04	0.09	0.58	0	0.22	0	0.05	5.34
Maharashtra	0.27	1.12	0.12	2.56	0	0.95	0	0.23	5.26
Andhra Pradesh	0.06	1.73	0.01	2.2	0	0.45	0	0.33	4.78
Karnataka	0	1.77	0.01	2.3	0	0.4	0.02	0.03	4.53
Assam	0.06	3.1	0	0.65	0	0.17	0	0.01	4
Madhya Pradesh	0.36	1.67	0	0.75	0	1.01	0	0.17	3.95
Orissa	0	1.17	0	0.81	0	0.61	0	0.09	2.68
Jharkhand	0.12	1.17	0.01	0.29	0	0.06	0	0	1.65
Haryana	0	0.5	0.01	0.35	0	0.52	0	0.08	1.46

Punjab	0	0.33	0	0.14	0	0.27	0	0.18	0.92
Uttaranchal	0	0.33	0	0.15	0	0.06	0	0.04	0.58
Jammu & Kashmir	0.04	0.15	0	0.28	0	0.01	0	0	0.49
Tamilnadu	0	0	0	0.36	0	0.06	0	0	0.42
Delhi	0	0	0	0	0.01	0.28	0	0	0.29
Chattisgarh	0	0.08	0	0.17	0	0.01	0	0	0.26
Meghalaya	0	0.16	0.02	0	0	0.04	0	0	0.23
Himachal Pradesh	0	0.05	0	0.07	0	0.03	0	0	0.15
Arunachal Pradesh	0.01	0.05	0.01	0.04	0	0.02	0.01	0	0.13
Chandigarh	0	0	0	0.06	0	0.03	0	0	0.09
Kerala	0	0.03	0	0	0	0	0	0.03	0.06
Nagaland	0	0.02	0	0.01	0	0.01	0	0	0.04
Dadra & Nagar Haveli	0	0.03	0	0	0	0	0	0	0.03
Manipur	0.01	0.01	0	0.01	0	0	0	0	0.02
Sikkim	0	0.01	0	0.01	0	0	0	0	0.02
Tripura	0	0	0	0.01	0	0	0	0	0.02
Pondicherry	0	0.01	0	0	0	0	0	0	0.01
Andaman & Nicobar islands	0	0	0	0	0	0	0	0	0
Daman & Diu	0	0	0	0	0	0	0	0	0
Goa	0	0	0	0	0	0	0	0	0
Lakshadweep	0	0	0	0	0	0	0	0	0
Mizoram	0	0	0	0	0	0	0	0	0
Total	4.03	47.12	3.45	32.14	0.22	9.46	0.17	3.39	100.0

Source: Unit Level Records of NSSO

DISTRIBUTION OF CHILD WORKERS BY MAJOR INDUSTRIES

The distribution of child workers by major industries is shown in table 2.4. It could be noted that the agriculture, hunting and forestry sector engaged over 90 per cent and 80 per cent of the child workers in the age group of 5-9 years and 10-14 years, respectively. Next in order of importance is the manufacturing sector accounting for about 7 per cent and 12 per cent of child workers in the age group of 5-9 years and 10-14 years, respectively. The other sectors employing the child workers include construction, hotels and restaurants, repair of motor vehicles and personal service. There were no child workers in the following industries:

- Electricity, gas and water supply
- Extra territorial organizations and bodies
- Financial intermediation
- Fishing
- Health and social work
- Mining and quarrying
- Public administration and defence; compulsory social security
- Real estate, renting and business activities

But, reports in the international media and press bring out evidences of the stark reality in the form of pictures of the children toiling in the mines (Agarwal, (2013). Thus, it is clear that even though we have very good laws in this country, their implementation is the real problem. Vandhana Kandhari, a child protection specialist at UNICEF, argues that there is a case for an exhaustive survey to capture child labour in India as NSSO surveys are not designed to serve this purpose in particular. India being a member of ILO can take assistance from Statistical Information and Monitoring Programme on Child Labour (SIMPOC), which is the statistical arm of **International Programme on the Elimination of Child labour** (IPEC). SIMPOC assists countries in the collection, documentation, processing and analysis of relevant data on child labour.

Table 2.4
Children in Workforce by Major Industries: NSSO
Survey, 2009-10 (Per cent)

Name of Industry	Child workers	
	5-9 years	10-14 years
Electricity, Gas and Water Supply	0	0
Other Community, Social and Personal Service Activities	0.48	0.5
Agriculture, Hunting and Forestry	90.17	79.89
Construction	0	2.59
Education	0	0.27
Extra territorial Organizations and Bodies	0	0
Financial Intermediation	0	0
Fishing	0	0
Health and Social Work	0	0
Hotels and Restaurants	1.98	1.81
Manufacturing	6.86	11.94
Mining and Quarrying	0	0
Public Administration and Defence; Compulsory Social Security	0	0
Real Estate Renting and Business Activities	0	0
Transport, Storage and Communications	0	0.26
Undifferentiated Production Activities of Private Households	0	0.01
Wholesale and Retail Trade; Repair of Motor Vehicles, Motorcycles	0.51	2.74
Total	100.00	100.00

Source: Unit Level Records of NSSO

Distribution of Child Workers by Enterprise

The distribution of child workers in the manufacturing sector by enterprise is shown in table 2.5. It may be seen that male and female proprietary

41

enterprise accounted for largest proportion of child workers in both the age groups of 5-9 years (47%) and 10-14 years (76%). The partnership enterprises with same household member and different household member stood second in terms of the proportion of child workers employed.

Table 2.5
Children in Workforce by Enterprise (%)

Name of Enterprise	Child workers	
	5-9 years	10-14 years
Co-operative societies/ trust/ other non-profit institutions	0	0
Employees Households	0	0.01
Female Proprietary	8.49	24.56
Govt./ Public Sector	0	0.98
Male Proprietary	38.04	50.98
Others	12.02	7.14
Partnership (With Different Household Member)	14.54	9.82
Partnership (With Same Household Member)	26.91	6.34
Public/ Pvt. Limited Company	0	0.17
Total	100.00	100.00

Now and then there are cases of exploitations of minor domestic helpers in the media, but where are they shown in the official statistics remains a big question. The stark reality is that it has been observed that bonded labour still prevails in many parts of India. There are many incidence of child labour cited in a working paper 'Bonded Labour in India: its Incidence and Pattern' by Ravi S. Srivastava (1996) and there are uncountable such incidents finding place in media almost daily. The bonded labour being an illegal practice is unlikely to be reported in NSSO survey. It calls for a more sophisticated survey to capture all the issues related to child labour. Besides, the NSSO survey shows that there are 11 per cent of children in the age group of 5-14 years who have never attended school or have discontinued the school for some reasons and there are 2 per cent of children in the same age group who are engaged in some or the other economic activity. This wide gap indicates serious underreporting of the child labour cases in the official statistics.

CHILD LABOUR FROM LOWER SOCIAL STRATA

It is evident that children who work belong to the lowest strata of society and children who stay out of school also belong to the lowest rung in the class structure. Acharya (1982), in a micro level study (4 villages from 2 districts) of child labour in West Bengal, found that out of the total non-enrolled children in the age-group 6-16, 70.34 per cent belong to the two lowest agrarian classes, namely poor peasants and agricultural labourers. It was also found that 92.23Percent of the total respondents belonging to the lower middle peasants, poor peasants and agricultural labourers who have non-enrolled children, maintained that their non-enrolled children were either gainfully employed or were engaged in household work like baby care, etc. A majority of the jotedars and rich peasants were against making elementary education a compulsory condition; Illiteracy among the labouring people, they generally think, will help them maintain the traditional authority pattern of village life. They feared that universal and compulsory enrolment would deprive them of the easy supply of child labour, which would lead to an increase in the cost of agricultural production.

LEGISLATION FOR ELIMINATING CHILD LABOUR IN INDIA

The first protective legislation for child labour in India was seen in 1881 in the form of Indian Factories Act, which had the provisions for prohibiting employment of children below 7 years, limiting the working hours for children to 9 hours a day and providing 4 holidays in a month and rest hours. This was actually made by the ruling British Government to decrease the production in Indian industries through some legal restrictions.

It may be mentioned here that the labour legislations in India including protective legislation for children have been greatly influenced by the result of various Conventions and Recommendations adopted by International Labour Organization. Besides Constitutional provisions, there are several legislative enactments, which provide legal protection to children in various occupations. The important legislations for eliminating child labour in India could be listed as follows:

- The Children (Pledging of Labour) Act, 1933
- The Employment of Children Act, 1938
- The Minimum Wages, Act 1948 and rules made thereunder by the government
- The Factories Act, 1948
- The Plantations Labour Act, 1951
- The Mines Act, 1952
- The Merchant Shipping Act, 1958
- The Motor Transport Workers' Act, 1961
- The Apprentices Act, 1961
- The Atomic Energy Act, 1962
- The Beedi and Cigar Workers (Conditions of Employment) Act, 1966
- The Shops and Establishment Act in Various States, and
- Child Labour (Prohibition and Regulation) Act, 1986

The Child Labour (Prohibition and Regulation) Act, 1986 was the culmination of efforts and ideas that emerged from the deliberations and recommendations of various committees on child labour. Significant among them were the National Commission on Labour (1966-69), the Gurupadaswamy Committee on Child Labour (1979) and the Sanat Mehta Committee (1984). The Act aims to prohibit the entry of children into hazardous

44

occupations and to regulate the services of children in non-hazardous occupations. In particular, it is aimed at (i) the banning of the employment of children, i.e., those who have not completed their 14th year, in 18 specified occupations and 65 processes; (ii) laying down a procedure to make additions to the schedule of banned occupations or processes; (iii) regulating the working conditions of children in occupations where they are not prohibited from working; (iv) laying down penalties for employment of children in violation of the provisions of this Act and other Acts which forbid the employment of children; (v) bringing uniformity in the definition of the child in related laws.

The Child Labour (Prohibition and Regulation) Amendment Bill, 2012 was introduced in Rajya Sabha on 4 December, 2012 further to amend the Child Labour (Prohibition and Regulation) Act, 1986. The amendment seeks a blanket ban on employing children below 18 years in hazardous industries like mining. The Bill is referred to Standing Committee on Labour and Employment.

JUDICIAL EFFORTS TOWARDS ENFORCEMENT OF CHILD LABOUR ACT, 1986

As per the data received from various states, the details of inspections carried out, prosecutions launched, convictions made under the Child Labour Act from 2007 to 2012 and current year are given in table 2.6. It may be noted that there was a progressive decline in the number of inspections conducted and prosecutions made from year to year between 2007 and 2012. Further, the number of convictions increased from 2007 to 2009 and thereafter declined gradually. The percentage of prosecutions to the inspections per year varied between 0.12 per cent and 5.4 per cent, while the percentage of convictions to prosecutions per year varied between 1.7 per cent and 28.4 per cent. On the whole, the percentage of prosecutions to inspections stood at 3.6 per cent, while the percentage of

45

convictions to prosecutions stood at 13.5 per cent. Thus, the effectiveness of implementation of Child Labour Act in terms of the percentage of prosecutions to inspections and the percentage of convictions to prosecutions could be termed low. It follows from the above discussion that many offenders are escaping punishment, while implementing the provisions of the Child Labour Act 1986, which calls for rigorous measures to effectively deal with the offenders in such cases.

Table-2.6
Year-wise Inspections, Prosecutions and Convictions under the Child Labour Act, 1986 in India

Year	No. of Inspections	No. of Prosecutions*	No. of Convictions**
2007	363927	12705 (0.12)	617 (4.9)
2008	355629	11318 (3.7)	763 (6.7)
2009	317083	11418 (3.6)	1312 (11.5)
2010	239612	8998 (3.8)	1308 (16.9)
2011	84935	4590 (5.4)	774 (1.7)
2012#	25040	589 (2.4)	167(28.4)
Total	1386226	49618 (3.6)	4941 (13.5)

Source: NCLP
Note: *Figures in the parentheses indicate percentages to the number of inspections in the respective years*
** Figures in the parentheses indicate percentages to the number of prosecutions in the respective years
# Information was not received from some states

On 10th December 1996 in Writ Petition (Civil) No.465/1986 on MC Mehta verses State of Tamil Nadu, the Supreme Court of India gave certain directions on the issue of elimination of child labour. The main features of judgment are as under:

• Survey for identification of working children;

46

- Withdrawal of children working in hazardous industry and ensuring their education in appropriate institutions;
- Contribution @ Rs.20,000/- per child to be paid by the offending employers of children to a welfare fund to be established for this purpose;
- Employment to one adult member of the family of the child so withdrawn from work, and, if that is not possible, a contribution of Rs.5,000/- to the welfare fund to be made by the State Government;
- Financial assistance to the families of the children so withdrawn to be paid -out of the interest earnings on the corpus of Rs.20,000/25,000 deposited in the welfare fund as long as the child is actually sent to the schools; and
- Regulating hours of work for children working in non-hazardous occupations so that their working hours do not exceed six hours per day and education for at least two hours is ensured. The entire expenditure on education is to be borne by the concerned employer.

The implementation of the direction of the Hon'ble Supreme Court is being monitored by the Ministry of Labour and compliance of the directions have been reported in the form of Affidavits on 05.12.97, 21.12.1999, 04.12.2000, 04.07.2001 and 04-12-2003 to the Hon'ble Court on the basis of the information received from the State/ UT Governments.

NATIONAL CHILD LABOUR PROJECT (NCLP)

In pursuance of the Child Labour Act 1986, the Government of India had launched the National Child Labour Project (NCLP) in 1988 to rehabilitate working children in 12 child labour endemic districts of the country. Its coverage has increased progressively to cover 271 districts in the country. As on date, the Scheme is in operation in 266 districts.

Under the NCLP, children are withdrawn form work and put into special schools, where they are provided with bridging education, vocational training, mid-day meal, stipend, health-care facilities, etc., and finally mainstreamed into the formal education system. At present, there are around 7,000 NCLP schools being run in the country with an enrolment of three lakh children. As per the estimates in 2013, more than 9 lakh working children have been mainstreamed to regular education under the NCLP.

The NCLP is a Central Sector scheme. Under the scheme, project societies are set up at the district level under the Chairpersonship of the Collector/ District Magistrate for overseeing the implementation of the project. Instructions to involve civil society and NGOs have also been issued.

The number of child labourers rescued, rehabilitated and mainstreamed through National Child Labour Project from 2009 to Dec 2012 in different States of the country is given in table 2.7. It may be seen that over 4 lakh child labourers were mainstreamed during the period from 2009 to 2012.

Table-2.7
State-wise Year-wise Child labour Mainstreamed

S. No	State	No. of Child labour Mainstreamed				
		2009-10	2010-11	2011-12	2012-13 (Up to Dec 2012)	Total
1	Assam	3685	274	227	10848	15034
2	Andhra Pradesh	13689	1858	13202	7840	36589
3	Bihar	7998	8552	19673	1162	37385
4	Chhattisgarh	1063	5164	4914	2004	13145
5	Gujarat	1437	2129	609	569	4744
6	Haryana	1354	1293	1895	1722	6264
7	Jammu & Kashmir	Nil	43	184	132	359
8	Jharkhand	1816	1015	2216	4003	9050
9	Karnataka	3217	135	3761	742	7855
10	Maharashtra	5150	5113	4532	4328	19123
11	Madhya Pradesh	9692	13344	17589	5044	45669
12	Orissa	10585	14416	13196	10309	48506
13	Punjab	1023	123	168	0	1314

14	Rajasthan	12326	4415	1020	4155	21916
15	Tamil Nadu	6321	6325	5127	3537	21310
16	Uttar Pradesh	40297	28243	29947	10617	109104
17	West Bengal	13187	2215	7456	3117	25975
	Total	132840	94657	125716	70129	423342

Source: Lok Sabha Starred Question No. 191 dated 11.3.2013

SCHOOL DROPOUT SCENARIO IN INDIA

The phenomenon of students discontinuing studies and repeating grades before completing elementary level of education is a major impediment in achieving Universalization of Elementary Education (UEE) in the country. In order to assess the impact school dropout on the achievement of UEE, it is necessary to estimate dropout and retention rates at primary and upper primary stages as well as transition rate from primary to upper primary and also the progress in this regard over time.

Available data relating to dropout rates indicate that during the period 2000-01 to 2008-09, the overall dropout rate for Classes I-V declined by 15.8 percentage points. The dropout rate for Classes I-VIII has declined by 11.4 percentage points during this period. There has been a steady decline in dropout rates in primary education since 2009-10. Between 2009-10 and 2012-13, the annual average dropout rate in primary education declined from 9.1 per cent to 4.7 per cent. The dropout rate, though declining from year to year, still remains a major challenge. The overall dropout rates in Classes I-V, Classes I-VIII and Classes I-X were 40.7 per cent, 53.7 per cent and 68.6 percent, respectively. The transition rate (from primary to upper primary stage) increased from 81.1 per cent in 2007-08 to 89.6 per cent in 2012-13.

The XI Five Year Plan (2007-2012) sought to reduce dropout rates in elementary education from 52.2 per cent in 2003-04 to 20 per cent by 2011-12; develop minimum standards of educational attainment in elementary school, and through regular testing monitor

49

effectiveness of education to ensure quality; increase literacy rate for persons of age 7 years and above to 85 per cent; lower gender gap in literacy to 10 percentage points; and increase the percentage of each cohort going to higher education from the present 10 per cent to 15 per cent by the end of the XI Plan.

The XII Five Year Plan (2012-2017) has accorded high priority to the expansion of education, ensuring that educational opportunities are available to all segments of the society, and ensuring that the quality of education imparted is significantly improved. The Twelfth Plan targets for school education and literacy include the following:

1. Ensuring universal access and, in keeping with the letter and spirit of the Right to Education (RTE) Act, 2009, providing good-quality free and compulsory education to all children in the age group of 6 to 14 years;

2. Improving attendance and reduce dropout rates at the elementary level to below 10 per cent and lower the percentage of out-of-school children (OoSC) at the elementary level to below 2 per cent for all socio-economic and minority groups and in all States/UTs;

3. Increasing enrolments at higher levels of education and raise the Gross Enrolment Ratio (GER) at the secondary level to over 90 per cent, at the higher secondary level to over 65 per cent;

4. Raising the overall literacy rate to over 80 per cent and reducing the gender gap in literacy to less than 10 per cent;

5. Providing at least one year of well-supported/well-resourced pre-school education in primary schools to all children, particularly those in educationally backward blocks (EBBs); and

6. Improving learning outcomes that are measured, monitored and reported independently at all levels of school education with a special focus on ensuring

that all children master basic reading and numeracy skills by Class II and skills of critical thinking, expression and problem solving by Class V.

Special Training for Mainstreaming of Out-of-school Children

The RTE Act makes specific provision for special training for age-appropriate admission for out-of-school children. During the year 2012-13, financial provision was made for providing special training to 2.8 million out-of-school children, including never-enrolled children and those who dropped out before completing elementary education.

Progress towards Universal Retention

One of the goals of the *Sarva Shiksha Abhiyan (SSA)* has been to achieve universal retention by enabling children enrolled in Class I to complete eight years of elementary education. The investment made in terms of expansion of schooling facilities, bridging gender and social category gaps in elementary education, and quality improvement initiatives, including improved school infrastructure, enhanced teacher availability, sustained academic support, Mid-day meal programme, awareness generation, increased community participation, curricular reforms and a rights-based approach, have contributed substantially to reduction in dropout rates and improved retention rates in primary, upper primary and elementary education.

Dropout Rate in Primary Education (Classes I-V)

Table 2.8 shows the dropout rates in primary education in India. It could be seen that during the period 2000-01 to 2008-09, the overall dropout rate for Classes I-V declined by 15.8 percentage points. The decline in dropout rates for girls (19 percentage points) was higher than that for boys (13 percentage points).

Table 2.8
Dropout Rates in Primary Education in India (all Categories of Students)

S. No	Year	Boys	Girls	Total
1	2000-01	39.7	41.9	40.7
2	2001-02	38.4	39.9	39
3	2002-03	35.9	33.7	34.9
4	2003-04	33.7	28.6	31.5
5	2004-05	31.8	25.4	29
6	2005-06	28.7	21.8	25.7
7	2006-07	24.6	25.7	25.6
8	2007-08	25.7	24.4	25.1
9	2008-09	26.7	22.9	24.9

Source: Statistics of School Education, 2007-08, MHRD, GoI; Educational Statistics at a Glance, 2011, MHRD, GoI.

Dropout Rate in Elementary Education (Classes I-VIII):

Table 2.9 shows the dropout rate in elementary education. It could be noted that the dropout rate for Classes I to VIII declined by 11.4 percentage points during the period from 2000-01 to 2008-09. The decline in dropout rates for girls (18.8 percentage points) was higher than that for boys (5.4 percentage points).

Table 2.9
Dropout Rates in Elementary Education in India (all Categories of Students Classes I-VIII)

S. No	Year	Boys	Girls	Total
1	2000-01	50.3	57.7	53.7
2	2001-02	52.9	56.9	54.6
3	2002-03	52.3	53.5	52.8
4	2003-04	51.9	52.9	52.3
5	2004-05	50.5	51.3	50.8
6	2005-06	48.7	49	48.8
7	2006-07	46.4	45.2	45.9
8	2007-08	43.7	41.3	42.7
9	2008-09	44.9	38.9	42.3

Source: Statistics of School Education, 2007-08, MHRD, GoI; Educational Statistics at a Glance, 2011, MHRD, GoI.

Dropout Rate in Primary and Elementary Education (SC students)

Table 2.10 presents the dropout rates in primary and elementary education for SC students. It could be seen that during the period 2000-01 to 2008-09, the overall dropout rate for SC students at primary stage (Classes I-V) declined by 18.5 percentage points. The overall dropout rate for SC students at the elementary stage (Classes I-VIII) declined by 12.8 percentage points during this period.

Table 2.10

Dropout Rates in Primary and Elementary Education (SC Students)

S. No	Year	Primary	Elementary
1	2001-02	45.2	60.7
2	2002-03	41.5	59.9
3	2003-04	36.6	59.4
4	2004-05	34.2	57.3
5	2005-06	32.9	55.2
6	2006-07	35.9	53.1
7	2007-08	30.1	52.5
8	2008-09	26.7	47.9

Source: Statistics of School Education, 2007-08, MHRD, GoI; Educational Statistics at a Glance, 2011, MHRD, GoI.

Dropout Rate in Primary and Elementary Education (ST students)

Table 2.11 shows the dropout rate in primary and elementary education for ST students. It may be noted that during the period 2000-01 to 2008-09, the overall dropout rate for ST students in primary education (Classes I-V) declined by 21 percentage points. The overall dropout rate for ST students in elementary education (Classes I-VIII) declined by 10.4 percentage points during this period.

Table- 2.11
Drop-out Rates in Primary and Elementary Education (ST Students)

S. No	Year	Primary	Elementary
1	2001-02	52.3	68.7
2	2002-03	51.4	68.7
3	2003-04	48.9	70.1
4	2004-05	42.3	65.9
5	2005-06	39.8	62.9
6	2006-07	33.1	62.5
7	2007-08	31.3	62.5
8	2008-09	31.3	58.3

Source: Statistics of School Education, 2007-08, MHRD, GoI; Educational Statistics at a Glance, 2011, MHRD, GoI.

Dropout rate by Grade/Class at Primary Level

Table 2.12 shows the dropout rate by grade/class at primary level. It could be seen that during the academic year 2009-10, 9.1 per cent of pupils at the primary stage of education (Classes I-V) had dropped out. The dropout rate was higher in Class I (10.2 per cent) and in Class V (15.9 per cent). There has been a steady decline in dropout rates in primary education since 2009-10. The annual average dropout rate in primary education declined by 4.4 per cent from 9.1 per cent in 2009-10 to 4.7 per cent in 2012-13. The decline in annual dropout rate was higher in Class I (5.4 per cent) and in Class V (6.4 per cent). The dropout rate, though declining from year to year, still remains a major challenge.

54

Table 2.12
Dropout rates by grade/class at primary level
(2009-10 & 2012-13)

Grade	Dropout rate (%)		
	2009-10	**2012-13**	**Decline (Percentage) points)**
Class I	10.2	4.8	5.4
Class II	6.7	2.3	4.4
Class III	7.2	3.6	3.6
Class IV	6.2	3.5	2.7
Class V	15.9	9.5	6.4
Primary Stage	9.1	4.7	4.4

Source: U-DISE (Unified District Information system for Education)NUEPA (National University of Educational Planning and Administration)

Transition to Upper Primary Education

A majority of primary schools do not have upper primary sections attached to them; consequently, many children have been dropping out after completing primary education. Opening of new upper primary sections/schools within reasonable walking distance from the habitations of residence of children has enabled children to continue their education beyond the primary stage. This has resulted in improvement in the transition rate. The transition rate has increased from 81.1 per cent in 2007-08 to 87.1 per cent in 2011-12 and then marginally declined to (chart 2.1) percent in 2012-13.

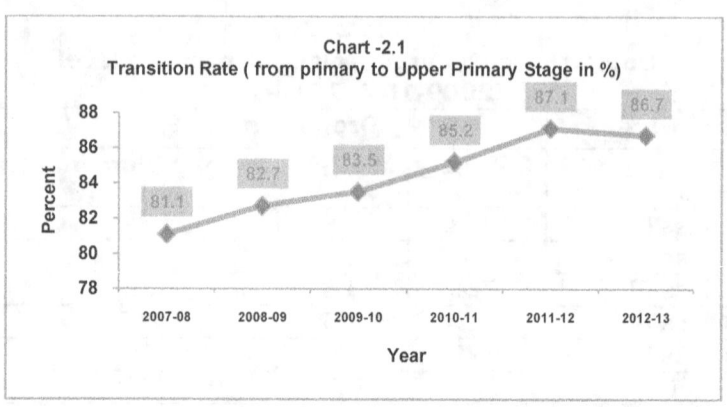

Chart -2.1
Transition Rate (from primary to Upper Primary Stage in %)

Source: U-DISE (Unified District Information system for Education) NUEPA (National University of Educational Planning and Administration)

Addressing the Residual Access and Equity Gaps in Elementary Education

The approach to addressing the residual access and equity gaps in elementary education will involve facilitating enrolment of out-of-school children, ensuring regular attendance of children enrolled in schools and tackling the problem of dropping out before completing the full cycle of elementary schooling, with special focus on girls and socially and economically disadvantaged groups. Key strategies include the following:

- Better targeting of out-of-school children through effective process of identification of these children, including an assessment of their current ability relating to reading, doing simple arithmetic and comprehension etc., enrolment of these children in regular schooling system, and introduction of accelerated learning strategies to mainstream these children into age-appropriate class.

- Provision of residential schools to reach out to children from vulnerable sections of society including children in areas of civil strife, children of migrating populations, children belonging to SC and ST;

- Providing residential facilities with special focus on ST children through conversion of at least five per cent of existing government elementary schools in all Educationally Backward Blocks (EBBs) with more than 50 per cent tribal population into Residential School Complexes (RSCs) having pre-school (non-residential), primary and upper primary sections.

- Special interventions for promoting education of SC children, including process-based interventions such as curricular review to include discussion on caste-based discrimination in textual material, residential schools run with assistance from the Ministry of Social Justice and Empowerment (MSJ&E), convergence on pre-matric scholarships and incentives provided by MSJ&E, and special efforts to ensure learning gains and completion of elementary cycle of education by children and continuation of education beyond elementary education.

- Promoting education of children with special needs (CWSN) through their identification and, placement in general schools, school readiness programmes, provision of aids and appliances, development and production of Braille books and construction of ramps and disabled-friendly toilets, and, through partnership with NGOs and competent private entities, designing curricula and implementation of the programme.

- Improving girls' education through the development of gender-sensitive curricula, pedagogical practices, teacher training and assessment of learning outcomes; making schools inclusive and safe; strengthening and expansion of KGBVs in Educationally Backward Blocks (EBBs), training of members of School Management Committees (SMCs) on gender and equity issues, and increased and more targeted investments for girls' education.

- Enhanced focus on educationally backward minorities by changing the unit of earmarking, targeting and monitoring of interventions for Muslim children from District to Block, and making specific activities of minority institutions, supported under the Ministry of Human Resource Development (MHRD) schemes, a part of the larger district plan prepared for minorities.
- Focused efforts in urban areas for enhancing access to elementary education by children of urban poor families.

Summing Up

To sum up, it may be said that there is an intricate relationship between the child labour and school dropout problems in India, and the efforts to overcome both the problems should go hand in hand to achieve significant results. Experience has shown that there is lack of coordination between the two, as a result of which both the problems still persist, especially in rural areas, and thereby pose serious challenges before the Nation. It is also important that the residual access and equity gaps in the elementary education are addressed in a comprehensive manner to overcome the problems of child labour and school dropout. Better targeting of out-of-school children, focusing on girls education and education of socially and economically backward sections of the society including minorities, focusing on educationally backward areas, and focusing on children with special needs are the need of the hour. Further, it is important that the on-going rural development and livelihood enhancement programmes are tied up with the programmes aimed at eliminating child labour and school dropout problems, together with the effective implementation of existing laws to achieve the goal of universalization of elementary education in the country.

References

Agarwal, (2013) "Child Labour in the Diamond Industry", International Labour Organization. pp. 51-53. *The New York Times*, February 26.

Jomo K.S. (1984) Early Labour: Children At Work On Malaysian Plantations. Kuala Lumpur and London: INSAN, the Institute for Social Analysis and Anti-Slavery Society for the Protection of Human Rights, p. 37.

Khatu, K.K et al: (1983) Working Children in India. Baroda: Operations Research Group, p. 69.

Kotwal, N.and Rani, S., "Causes of School Dropouts among Rural Girls in Kathua District", *Journal of Human Ecology*, Vol.22, No.1, July 2007, pp. 57-59.

Mehta, Arun C (2008). "Elementary Education in India: Progress towards UEE", New Delhi: NUEPA.

Mohinder Singh: (1987-88) "Planning and Performance. Closing the Gap In Primary Education", Future. Development Perspective on Children. 22-23, Winter, New Delhi: UNICEF, p. 29.

Naik J.P (1975) Equality, *"Quality and Quantity:The elusive triangle in Indian Education"*, New Delhi: A1 lied Publishers Private Limited, p. 117.

Neera Burra, (1987) A Report on Child Labour in the Gem Polishing Industry of Jaipur, Rajasthan, India. New Delhi: prepared for UNICEF, October, mimeo, p. 37.

Poromesh Acharya, (1982) "Child Labour". *Seminar,* 275, July, pp. 18-19.

Rani, U.R., "Reasons For Rising School Dropout Rates Of Rural Girls In India- An Analysis Using Soft Computing Approach", *International Journal of Current Research*, Vol.3, No.9, January 2011, pp.140-143

Ravi and srivastava (1996), Agrarian Change and the Labour Process, in Peter Robb (ed), Meaning of Agriculture, New Delhi: IXFORD University Press, PP.132-5.

Rupon Basumatary, "School Dropout across Indian States and UTs: An Econometric Study", *International Research Journal of Social Sciences*, Vol. 1, No.4, December 2012, pp. 28-35.

CHAPTER-III
MAINSTREAMING OF SCHOOL DROPOUTS IN ANDHRA PRADESH WITH SPECIAL REFERENCE TO KURNOOL DISTRICT

INTRODUCTION

The government of India initiated specific measures under the National Child Labour Project (NCLP) in child labour endemic districts of the country to mainstream the out-of-school children including school dropouts and never enrolled children by enrolling them either directly or through bridge courses (residential and non-residential) into the formal schooling system. In view of the fact that the out-of-school children are the potential child labour, the Government of Andhra Pradesh followed an integrated approach to tackle these twin problems by effecting convergence with various departments. In this chapter, an attempt is made to examine the process of mainstreaming the school dropouts in Andhra Pradesh with special reference to Kurnool district. Before doing so, this chapter provides a review on the role of education in human development, and how investments are made on education and the impact of such investments on literacy rates in India. This chapter also provides a critical analysis of educational status of Andhra Pradesh state in terms of literacy rates across the districts, schooling facilities, teacher-pupil ratio, enrolment rate, dropout rates, etc., over time. Besides, this chapter provides a brief account on the profile of Kurnool district and discusses the efforts made towards mainstreaming of school dropouts through NCLP.

ROLE OF EDUCATION IN HUMAN DEVELOPMENT

Education is a key to sustainable development. For peace and stability within and among the countries witnessing rapid globalization, education is an indispensable means to ensure effective participation of people in the economic activities. While traditionally 'Education' has meant children in schools, it is equally important to address the learning needs of adults. Combining these two components of the learning continuum, most countries have enlarged the scope of educational planning to include basic education and adult literacy to achieve 'Education for all'. As per the article 21A and 93rd Constitutional Amendment in 2009, 'Education' has become a fundamental right. The article 21A clearly spells out the responsibility of the State to the extent of providing free and compulsory education to all the children in the age of 6 to 14 years. The government is committed to achieve total literacy by 2015 and in this direction initiated several schemes.

Education has a pivotal role to guide and induce a person to the process of self-realization. An educated person carries autonomous and authentic ideas and not the one who has been conditioned or indoctrinated. Education puts one on to the path of meaningful learning and realizing. It expected that education would improve the quality of life of a person to behave in a better manner than one who is not educated. There is a sense of being let down, disappointment and dismay if an educated person cannot conduct himself in a manner that is rational, morally good and socially responsible. It is clear that education is meant for an all-round development of a person, not merely specialization or professional training. Educationists too stress that education is a holistic process and not only a training of the intellect. It is the development of moral, social, aesthetic as well as rational capacity. People might differ on the degree of importance that they place on these various dimensions but most would include all these in their notion of an educated person.

Educational facilities definitely promote the prosperity of the society and contribute positively to gross domestic product and create employment opportunities. It has a positive effect on reduction of poverty, population growth, crime rate and better health condition.

The knowledge possessed by the population and their capacity and training to use it effectively is also very important. Expenditure on education, training and research can contribute to the productivity by raising the quality of the workforce, and these outlays yield a counting return in future. If this expenditure were considered as expenditure on capital then the proportion of capital formation in the national income of rich countries would be much higher. But since poor countries do not make huge investments in the formation of human capital, national income would not increase significantly in proportion to the expenditure incurred on education.

While investment on human resources has been witnessing a high growth in advanced countries, the negligible amount of human investment in developing countries has done little to extend the capacity of the people to meet the challenges of accelerated development. The characteristic of "economic backwardness" is still manifest in several ways like low labour efficiency, factor immobility, limited specialization in occupations and in trade, a deficient supply of entrepreneurship, and customary values and traditional social institutions that minimize the incentives for economic change. It has to be recognized that the wrong kind of education unaccompanied by the required complementary actions can check or reverse the process of development.

INVESTMENTS ON EDUCATION IN INDIA

Education continues to be a neglected part of planning of India in mitigating the contemporary problems for the efficient utilization of human resources. To attract the downtrodden such as SCs, STs, minorities and women, it is essential to allocate more funds for the establishment, expansion and strengthening of educational facilities like appointment of teachers, infrastructure, equipment, drinking water, sanitation, compound wall, play ground, library, etc., in

62

rural areas. The existing edge of challenge is in rural schools. More than a century ago, Jyothirao Phule wrote in his moving appeal to the Hunter Commission (1984) that conditions in rural schools were terrible.

The Government of India quantitatively forced a target of investing 6 per cent of national income on education on the recommendation of the Education Commission (1966). The Kothari Commission also suggested that a higher (more than 6 per cent) investment would need to be allocated on education in India (1986). But the goal remains elusive even today. This is one of the glaring promises that continue to remain a goal repeatedly postponed, unfulfilled and often reiterated.

The proportion of GNP invested on education in many other developing countries including India is very low as compared to other developed countries of the world. According to Human Development Report, 2004, India's was ranked 78th out of 137 countries. India was spending 4.1 per cent of her GNP on education (1999-2001). In comparison, a large number of countries spend more than 6-8 per cent and some of them even more than 10 per cent on education. Expenditure on education influences literacy levels (Sharif and Ghosh, 2000). The share of elementary education in the total expenditure on education continues to be below 50 per cent as against the required 65-70 per cent to achieve universal literacy.

LITERACY RATES IN INDIA: 1951-2011

In a country like India, literacy is the main foundation for social and economic growth. When the British rule ended in India in the year 1947 the literacy rate was just 12%. Over the years, India has changed socially, economically, and globally. As per the 2011 Census, literacy rate India was found to be 74.04 per cent. Compared to the adult literacy rate, the youth literacy rate is about 9 per cent higher. Though this seems like a very great accomplishment, it is still a matter of concern that so many people in India cannot even read and write. The numbers of children who do not get education, especially in the rural areas, are still high. Though the government has made a law that every child under the age of 14 should get free education, the problem of illiteracy is still large.

Table 3.1 shows the literacy rates in India in all the Census operations after the country achieved Independence, i.e., from 1951 to 2011, including the gender gap in literacy. It is clear from table 3.1 that from 1951 Census to 2011 Census the literacy rates have shown substantial improvement. The literacy rate, which was only 18.33 per cent in 195, rose to 52.21 per cent in 1991 and further increased to 74.04 per cent in 2011. According to 2011 Census, the literacy rate has gone up to 82.14 per cent for males and 65.46 per cent for females. Interestingly, literacy rate improved sharply among females as compared to males between 2001 and 2011; while the effective literacy rate for males rose from 75.26 to 82.14 per cent marking a rise of 6.9 per cent, it increased by 11.8 per cent for females from 53.67 to 65.46 per cent. It could also be noted that the gender gap in literacy rate has increased from 1951 to 1981 with some fluctuations in between, but has declined steadily thereafter. The decline in gender gap in literacy rate was highest between 2001 and 2011. On the whole, the gender gap in literacy rate increased from 18.5 per cent in 1951 to 26.62 per cent in 1981, but declined to 16.68 per cent in 2011.

TABLE – 3.1
Literacy Rates in India 1951-2011 (Percent)

Census Year	Persons	Male	Females	Gender gap in literacy rate
1951	18.33	27.16	8.66	18.5
1961	28.3	40.4	15.35	25.05
1971	34.45	45.96	21.97	23.98
1981	43.57	56.38	29.76	26.62
1991	52.21	64.13	39.29	24.84
2001	65.38	75.26	54.16	21.7
2011	74.04	82.14	65.46	16.68

Source: Registrar General, Census of India
* Provisional data of the 2011 census
In order to fulfil the Constitutional obligation of providing compulsory education to all children aged 6-14 years, India has launched the programme of Sarva Shiksha Abhiyan in 2000-01 to achieve Universalization of Elementary Education in the country by the year 2010. It implies that all children in the age group of 6 to14 years get enrolled in a regular school or an alternative school system and they do not drop out from school before completing the full cycle of elementary education. Efforts are being made on various fronts to ensure that no child in this age group remains out of school. The programme is an effort towards recognition of the need for improving the performance of the school system through a community owned approach and ensuring quality elementary education in a mission mode to all children, and also seeks to bridge gender and social gaps.

EDUCATIONAL STATUS OF ANDHRA PRADESH

Since the reference period of the study relates to undivided Andhra Pradesh, the data presented on the State pertains to Andhra Pradesh as existed before June 2, 2014. The educational status of the State is examined here in terms of literacy rates across the districts, education facilities, children in schools, number of schools, number of teachers,

Literacy Rates across the Districts: 1991 to 2011

A person, who is 7 years and above and who is able to read and write with understanding in any one language is considered as 'Literate'. The literacy rate of the state is 67.66 per cent in 2011 as against 44.08 per cent in 1991. The literacy rate of the state is lower than that of all India literacy rate (74.04 per cent) in 2011. Among the districts, Hyderabad is at the top with 80.96 per cent. The least literate district is Mahabubnagar with 56.06 per cent. Male literacy rate is 75.56 per cent as against that of females at 59.74 per cent in 2011. District-wise literacy rates are given in table 3.2.

65

Table – 3.2
Educational Facilities in Andhra Pradesh from 1996-97 to 2011-12

Year	Primary Schools			Upper Primary Schools			High Schools			Higher Secondary Schools		
	Sc.	En.	Teac.	Sc.	En.	Teac.	Sc.	En.	Teac.	Sc.	En.	Teac.
1996-97	48899	5635379	106974	7733	2130398	50287	8178	3505246	107506	93	99848	4365
1997-98	49919	5936750	121446	8142	2274897	58509	8566	3617222	112850	95	96131	4387
1998-99	51836	6237735	136363	8713	2443179	62845	8897	3767758	115670	97	101850	4654
1999-00	55398	6373837	136853	9530	2614524	69117	9659	4177431	122891	88	92292	4154
2000-01	55901	6060394	133546	9804	2628185	69265	10277	4537791	131324	82	82227	3847
2001-02	58249	5230748	127313	14472	3322826	85263	11464	4963392	145246	73	74765	3498
2002-03	63362	6351072	173731	15110	3389189	102152	12570	4078358	140019	79	78336	3628
2003-04	63897	5967010	172601	15215	3149964	100365	13160	4330479	140826	82	82033	3305
2004-05	61680	5524363	166935	16667	3172877	103985	14342	4633242	140399	79	80586	3475
2005-06	62159	5398008	166790	17290	3172134	106215	15437	4839243	142544	98	102538	3958
2006-07	62162	5513155	167723	17823	3246096	112388	16195	4988791	153988	97	103188	4056
2007-08	62464	5366949	167059	17957	3110686	110949	16937	5114442	156887	99	99664	4241
2008-09	65609	5686045	183197	14942	2492198	94662	17376	5369962	167159	100	110955	4127
2009-10	65932	5392253	169159	15384	2395849	90077	18143	5477427	187709	104	100827	4147
2010-11	66834	5463896	174069	15421	2329730	93003	18776	5397690	205179	173	126870	4304
2011-12	66721	5276876	189722	15759	2157321	97015	19770	5407778	204060	186	138863	4314

Source: *School Education Department,*
Note: *Sc.= No. of Schools; En. = Enrolment; Teac. = Teachers*

Table – 3.3
Literacy Rates by Sex across the Districts in Andhra Pradesh

S. No.	District	Males			Females			Total		
		1991	2001	2011	1991	2001	2011	1991	2001	2011
1	Adilabad	45.05	64.98	71.22	20.60	40.30	51.99	32.96	52.68	61.55
2	Nizamabad	47.33	64.91	72.66	21.35	39.48	52.33	34.18	52.02	62.25
3	Karimnagar	50.79	67.09	74.72	23.37	42.75	55.18	37.17	54.90	64.87
4	Medak	45.15	64.33	72.50	19.25	38.66	52.49	32.41	51.65	62.53
5	Hyderabad	78.90	83.74	83.35	63.56	73.50	78.42	71.52	78.80	80.96
6	Ranga Reddy	60.43	75.26	84.00	36.91	56.49	71.82	49.07	66.16	78.05
7	Mahabubnagar	40.80	56.63	66.27	18.03	31.89	45.65	29.58	44.41	56.06
8	Nalgonda	50.53	69.23	74.94	24.92	44.68	55.05	38.00	57.15	65.05
9	Warangal	51.98	68.88	75.91	26.08	45.09	56.45	39.30	57.13	66.16
10	Khammam	50.04	66.11	73.20	30.53	47.44	57.85	40.50	56.89	65.46
11	Srikakulam	49.14	67.19	72.25	23.52	43.68	52.56	36.22	55.31	62.59
12	Vizianagaram	45.93	62.37	69.04	22.47	39.91	50.16	34.19	51.07	59.49
13	Visakhapatnam	56.13	69.68	75.48	34.60	50.12	60.00	45.51	59.96	67.70
14	East Godavari	55.32	70.00	74.91	42.26	60.94	67.82	48.79	65.48	71.35
15	West Godavari	59.75	78.05	77.63	46.98	68.99	71.05	53.38	73.53	74.32
16	Krishna	60.55	74.39	79.13	45.54	63.19	69.62	53.16	68.85	74.37
17	Guntur	56.54	71.24	75.40	35.85	53.74	60.64	46.35	62.54	67.99
18	Prakasam	53.14	69.35	73.54	27.06	45.08	53.40	40.30	57.38	63.53
19	Nellore	58.04	73.67	75.93	36.99	56.38	62.30	47.61	65.08	69.15
20	Kadapa	63.14	75.83	78.41	32.35	49.54	57.26	48.12	62.83	67.88
21	Kurnool	53.24	65.96	71.36	26.04	40.03	50.81	39.97	53.22	61.13
22	Anantapur	55.92	68.38	74.09	27.61	43.34	54.31	42.18	56.13	64.28
23	Chittoor	62.61	77.62	81.15	36.44	55.78	63.65	49.75	66.77	72.36
	ANDHRA PRADESH	55.12	70.32	75.56	32.72	50.43	59.74	44.08	60.47	67.66

Source: *Census of India, 2001, Director of Census Operations, Andhra Pradesh.* & Census of India 2011(provisional figures)

66

Schooling Facilities

The Directorate of School Education deals with School Education catering to the educational needs of children. The pattern of School Education in Andhra Pradesh is 5+2+3 i.e., 5 years of Primary Education, 2 years of Upper Primary Education and 3 years of Secondary Education. The Govt. of Andhra Pradesh envisaged intends to achieve the goal of universalization of elementary education by recognizing education as a potential instrument for human development. The primary goal of the state is to increase steadily the overall literacy levels. Provision of schooling facilities within a distance of 1 km. of all rural habitations is a pre-requisite for achieving universal access. For this, Primary Schools are started in almost all places within a distance of 1 km.

The educational facilities in terms of the number of schools, enrolment in schools and number of teachers from 1996-97 to 2011-12 is shown in table 3.3. It may be seen that there has been a growth in the number of primary schools to the tune of 36.4 per cent between 1996-97 and 2011-12, while the corresponding figure with regard to the number of teachers in primary schools stood at 77.4 per cent. Surprisingly, the enrolment in primary schools recoded a negative growth of -6.4 per cent during the same period. Similarly, the number of schools and teachers in upper primary schools increased by 103.8 per cent and 92.9 per cent, respectively, while the enrolment recorded only a marginal increase of just 1.3 per cent.

Number of Schools

Out of 1,02,436 schools in Andhra Pradesh in 2011-12, there were 66,721 Primary Schools (65%) and 15,759 Upper Primary Schools (15%) in the Elementary Education sector. Under Secondary Education there were 19,770 High Schools and 186 Higher Secondary Schools. Out of the total of 1,02,436 schools, 114 were Central Government schools, 7,716 State Government,

67

66,393 MP/ZP, 2,115 Municipal, 3,335 Private Aided and 22,763 Private Unaided. The schools managed by the government including PRIs accounted for 74.5 per cent of the total schools in the state. On the other hand, the private aided schools accounted for 3.3 per cent, while the private unaided schools accounted for 22.2 per cent of total schools in the state. Thus, 78 per cent of the schools are under the direct control of the government. The state government exercises indirect control even on the private unaided schools by imposing certain terms and conditions, but to a limited extent only. There is no control of the government on fees structure in private aided and unaided schools.

Number of Teachers

During 2011-12, there were 4,95,138 teachers in position in all types of schools in the state, out of which 1,89,722 in primary schools (38.3%) , 97,015 in upper primary schools (19.6%), 2,04,060 in High schools (41.2%) and 4,314 teachers in higher secondary schools (0.9%). The Government has been making efforts to achieve teacher pupil ratio of 1:40. The percentage pass of students in S.S.C examinations during 2009-10 is 81.63, which is higher than the previous year pass of 78.8 Percent.

Teacher-Pupil Ratio

A major element of the approach to strengthening education will be to improve current learning levels by lowering the teacher pupil ratio. The Government has been striving hard to achieve teacher-pupil ratio of 1:40. The Teacher Pupil Ratios for Primary, Upper Primary and High Schools are shown in Table- 3.4, from which it becomes evident that the teacher-pupil ratios were brought down below the desired level right from 2002-03 onwards in all categories of schools.

Table – 3.4
Teacher Pupil Ratios in Andhra Pradesh

Year	Primary	Upper Primary	High School
2000-01	45	38	34
2001-02	41	39	34
2002-03	37	33	29
2003-04	35	31	31
2004-05	29	25	30
2005-06	28	25	30
2006-07	29	24	29
2007-08	28	23	28
2008-09	27	22	29
2009-10	28	23	28

Source: School Education Department

Dropout Rates

Dropout rate is defined as the percentage of the number of children to total enrolment dropping out of the educational system in a particular year. The dropout rate does not take into account repeaters and children who enter the system after class-I. It is expected that every child who enters class-I completes class-VII without discontinuing the school in between. With this view, efforts are being made to tackle the problem of dropouts with the support of School Management Committees. The Dropout Rate during 2011-12 stood at 15.60 per cent in Primary Stage (Classes I-V) 20.79 per cent in Upper Primary Stage (Classes I-VII), and 45.71 per cent in Secondary Schools stage. The details of Dropout rates in Andhra Pradesh from 1971-72 to 2011-12 are shown in table-3.5, from which it becomes evident that the dropout rates have shown a steady decline over time, especially from 2003-04 onwards at all stages.

69

Table – 3.5
Dropout Rates in Andhra Pradesh from 1971-72 to 2011-12

Year	Class I – V			Class I – VII			Class I – X		
	Boys	Girls	Total	Boys	Girls	Total	Boys	Girls	Total
1971-72	69.34	72.53	70.65	77.80	86.91	81.59	87.62	94.37	90.56
1981-82	58.48	62.87	60.31	64.40	73.19	67.98	78.28	85.91	81.35
1991-92	52.15	57.04	54.28	61.17	69.17	64.65	72.76	79.31	75.54
2001-02	35.36	33.64	34.54	51.98	55.77	53.78	71.62	73.28	72.37
2003-04	42.42	42.80	42.61	52.71	55.92	54.27	65.28	68.53	66.70
2004-05	31.77	32.14	31.95	51.96	54.46	53.17	62.30	65.24	63.69
2005-06	24.61	24.85	24.73	50.26	52.37	51.30	62.24	65.20	63.67
2006-07	26.76	27.32	27.04	42.14	44.32	43.22	62.99	65.33	64.13
2007-08	19.10	18.48	18.79	33.26	35.23	34.24	62.30	64.00	63.13
2008-09	16.14	15.15	15.65	34.39	35.41	34.89	60.12	61.38	60.73
2009-10	16.34	15.24	15.80	26.38	26.50	26.44	52.73	54.2	53.36
2010-11	18.10	16.73	17.43	22.56	22.11	22.34	45.83	46.59	46.21
2011-12	15.93	15.27	15.60	21.51	20.06	20.79	45.43	45.99	45.71

Source: School Education Department

Enrolment

Steps are being taken to enrol all the out-of-school children and to free the children working in the domestic sector and other organizations. As a result of the enrolment drive in the name of 'Badi Bata' from 1st - 16th June 2006 onwards to enrol all school age children, as many as 14.41 lakh children (5+) were enrolled into class-I. About 1.64 lakh out of school children were enrolled into regular/ bridge schools. About 1.341 lakh of children were enrolled in 522 Residential bridge courses and 3,063 Alternative and Innovative Education (AIE) centres. Innovative strategies and interventions of the Government resulted in a considerable increase in enrolment and retention. The strategy for achieving universal participation involves strengthening of the existing infrastructure, opening new primary schools, establishment of alternative schools and other types of educational facilities in smaller and un-served habitations. Due to these interventions and several other programmes, enrolment has increased in all stages of education. Total enrolment during 2011-12 was 129.81 lakhs in schools, out of which 52.77 lakhs (40.7%) were in Primary Schools, 21.58 lakhs (16.6%) and 54.08 lakhs (41.7%) were in Upper Primary and High Schools respectively, and the remaining in Higher Secondary Schools.

Mid-Day Meal Programme

In order to bring back the children into schools and retain them in schools for achieving the objective of 'Education for All' and to provide nutritious food to the children for their physical and mental development, Midday Meal Programme (MDP) is being implemented from January 2003 in the state. Under the scheme, a minimum content of 450 calories and 12 grams of protein content is provided per child on each working day of the school for classes I to V and 700 calories and 20 grams of protein content is provided per child on each working day of the school for classes VI to X. The children of Classes I - X studying in Primary, Upper Primary and High Schools of Government/ Local bodies and Aided institutions are covered under this scheme. Under the MDP, an amount of Rs. 597.29 crores, has been spent during 2007-08 to 2010-11 (till Dec.2011). The amount includes the state contribution besides the Central allocation. Under the scheme, 60.33 lakh students during 2007-08, 70.44 lakh students during 2008-09, 70.43 lakh students during 2009-10 and 74.44 lakhs students during 2010-11 have been covered. The Govt. of India is providing rice free of cost @ 100 grams per child per working day. The conversion cost is paid to the identified implementing agencies towards cooking cost.

Sarva Shiksha Abhiyan

Under the SSA programme, an amount of Rs.3134.68 crores was spent during the last four years 2007-08 to 2010-11(till Dec.2011) in Andhra Pradesh. Under this scheme, during the 4-year period, 210 new school buildings have been constructed, 170 schools have been made operational. Further, several schools have been provided with adequate drinking water facility and toilet facility. Due to the infrastructure facilities created and academic support, there has been improvement in enrolment as well as reduction in dropout rates.

Community Participation (School Management Committee)

For the first time in the country, the Govt. of Andhra Pradesh has enacted "Community Participation Act 1998" involving the community in school management. Resources are transferred to School Committees empowering them to plan, manage and promote quality education. In terms of 73rd and 74th Constitutional Amendments, Sarpanches/ Ward members have been made the Chairpersons of the School Management Committees.

Vidya Volunteers

In view of the large number of representations received from School Management Committees seeking Government support to achieve Universalization of Primary Education and duly taking into account the inadequate teacher-pupil ratio, the Government of Andhra Pradesh decided to support School Management Committees to provide 'Vidya Volunteers'. The Government decided to provide financial assistance on purely temporarily basis to School Management Committees to enlist Vidya Volunteers by them on contract basis.

District Institute of Education and Training (DIET)

The Government of Andhra Pradesh has upgraded 23 Teacher Training Institutes as District Institutes of Education and Training and one Tribal Teachers Training Institute at Utnoor as Sub-DIET in a phased manner. In 13 DIETs, Urdu medium parallel sections are functioning and 65 lecturer posts have been sanctioned. The Tamil medium parallel section with intake of 50 is functioning at DIET, Chittoor at Karvetinagar.

Besides, the Government is implementing Computer Education Programme under BOOT Model through seven agencies in 5,000 High schools from 2008-09 for 5 years and in 1,300 High schools from 2010-11 for 5 years to improve the enrolment and retention rates.

PROFILE OF KURNOOL DISTRICT

Kurnool District is located in the west-central part of Andhra Pradesh on the southern banks of the Tungabhadra and Handri rivers. The Kurnool city is the headquarters of the district, and served as the first capital of erstwhile Andhra state. It is known as the 'Gateway of Rayalaseema'.

Physical Characteristics

The boundaries of Kurnool district are Guntur and Nellore districts on the East, Bellary district on the West, Mahaboob Nagar district on the North, Kadapa and Anantapur district on the South. The total area of the district is 17,658 sq.km, which accounts for 6.42 Percent of total area of Andhra Pradesh and 26.26 Percent of total area of the Rayalaseema region. There are 920 villages with 894 inhabited and 26 uninhabited villages in the district.

Kurnool falls under scarce rainfall zone (VI) with a Normal rainfall of 670 mm per annum, of which nearly 68 Percent is being received from South West monsoon and 22 Percent during North East monsoon Period. Rainfall in Kurnool is mostly erratic, insufficient and unevenly distributed. Hence, drought or floods is a common phenomenon. The major rivers of the district are Tungabhadra, Handri, Krishna, Kunderu and Gundlakamma.

Trade and Commerce

The most important commodity manufactured and exported is groundnut oil while the most important commodity imported is pulses. Kurnool city is a trading centre for agricultural products like groundnut, cotton, corn, etc.

73

Types of Soils

The soils in the district are classified as clay, loamy and sandy soils. The black cotton soils are predominant in the mandals of Pattikonda, Nandyal, Allagadda, Koilkuntla, Nadikotkur and Adoni. In the eastern part of the district, red soil of a poor quality largely predominates. These soils, although generally poor in fertility, yield a very good crop with a minimum rainfall.

Administration

At present the district consists of 54 mandals spread over three revenue divisions, viz., Kurnool, Nandyal and Adoni. The map of Kurnool district with Mandals has been given in the figure 3.1.

Fig.3.1
Map of Kurnool District Showing Mandals/ Tehsils

74

Industries

In Kurnool district, there are large-scale and medium-scale industries with an investment of Rs.51,017.72 lakhs. The number of small-scale units are 18,852 providing employment to 46,465 workers with an investment of Rs.19,757.72 lakhs. There are 777 factories with a working capital of Rs.6,206 lakhs.

Tourism

The important religious centres in the district are Srisailam, Mahanandi, Ahobilam, Yaganti. The historic places are Konda Reddy Buruju at Kurnool town and Belum Caves in Banaganapalli mandal and Rolla Padu Sanctuary, which attract a number of tourists.

Demographic Particulars

In 2011, Kurnool had population of 4,053,463, comprising 2,039,227 males and 2,014,236 females, the sex ratio being 988 females per 1000 males. However, the child sex ratio worked out to 938 girls per 1000 boys. The population of Kurnool District constituted 4.79 per cent of State's total population. About 28.35 per cent of the population lives in urban areas, with the majority of population residing in rural areas, as per the 2011 Census. There was a growth of 14.85 per cent in the population in 2011 compared to population in 2001. The district had a population density of 230 persons per sq. km as per the 2011 Census.

Table-3.6
Demographic Particulars of Kurnool District:2001-2011

Description	2011	2001
Actual Population	4,053,463	3,529,494
Male	2,039,227	1,796,214
Female	2,014,236	1,733,280
Population Growth	14.85%	18.72%
Area Sq. Km	17,658	17,658
Density/km2	230	200

Proportion to Andhra Pradesh Population	4.79%	4.63%
Sex Ratio (Per 1000)	988	965
Child Sex Ratio (0-6 Age)	938	958
Average Literacy	59.97	53.22
Male Literacy	70.1	65.96
Female Literacy	49.78	40.03
Total Child Population (0-6 Age)	506,239	537,606
Male Population (0-6 Age)	261,217	274,560
Female Population (0-6 Age)	245,022	263,046
Literates	2,127,161	1,592,172
Male Literates	1,246,369	1,003,659
Female Literates	880,792	588,513
Child Proportion (0-6 Age)	12.49%	15.23%
Boys Proportion (0-6 Age)	12.81%	15.29%
Girls Proportion (0-6 Age)	12.16%	15.18%

Source:
1. Hand book of Statistics, Kurnool district-2006-07
2. Registrar General census of India for 2011 population.

The average literacy rate of Kurnool district in 2011 was 59.97 per cent compared to 53.22 per cent in 2001. The male and female literacy rates were 70.10 per cent and 49.78 per cent respectively. The district stood at the lowest position in Rayalaseema region in terms of literacy rate. The demographic particulars of Kurnool district as per the 2001 and 2011 Census are presented in table 3.6.

EDUCATIONAL FACILITIES IN KURNOOL DISTRICT

The Kurnool district is well endowed with good number of educational institutions ranging from pre-primary schools to university. Besides the district is the centre for medical and engineering education.

Growth of Schools

The growth of schools in Kurnool district during 2005-06 to 2011-12 is presented in table 3.7.

Table-3.7
Schools in Kurnool District by Management from 2005-06 to 2011-12

Year	CG	SG	MPP/ZPP	MPL	PA	PUA	Total
2005-06	3	137	2432	137	178	616	3503
2006-07	3	142	2422	137	183	679	3566
2007-08	2	130	2424	137	185	681	3559
2008-09	2	140	2423	137	179	705	3586
2009-10	2	149	2423	137	178	718	3607
2010-11	2	166	2489	140	178	813	3788
2011-12	2	178	2489	140	174	919	3902

Note: CG = Central government; SG = State government; MPP/ZPP = PRIs;
MPL = Municipality; PA = Private Aided; and PUA = Private Unaided
Source: 1.Commissioner and Director of School
Education, State Project Director RVM (SSA)
2. District Educational Office, Kurnool

It may be noted from table 3.7 that the total number of schools in the Kurnool district gradually increased between 2005-06 and 2011-12. In 2005-06, there were 3503 schools in the district, which increased to 3902 in 2011-12, i.e., by 11.4 per cent. On an average, 66 schools were started per year in the district. The schools under the Central Government management stood at 3 up to 2006-07, but were reduced to 2 from 2007-08 onwards. The State Government schools also gradually increased from year to year, except in 2007-08. The increase in State Government schools per year worked out to 29.8 per cent during the above period. A large number of schools in the district are under the management of Mandal Praja Parishad and Zilla Praja Parishad. The percentage of schools under Mandal Praja Parishad and Zilla Praja Parishad in 2011-12 constituted 63.8 per cent of total schools in the district. The number of schools under

77

Mandal Praja Parishad and Zilla Praja Parishad management increased by 11.4 per cent during the above period. There was no growth in number of schools under municipal management up to 2009-10. In 2010-11, 3 new additional schools were added under municipal management. With regard to private aided schools there is negative growth. The number of private aided schools declined after 2007-08. The main reason for this phenomenon is that the government decided to wind up those private aided schools for want of minimum students' strength. However, the number of private unaided schools increased by 49.2 per cent during the above period.

Trends in Enrolment

The enrolment trends of both boys and girls in Kurnool district are presented in table 3.8. It is evident from table 3.9 that the total strength in Central Government schools is not evenly distributed. The highest strength was registered

Table – 3.8
Management-wise Enrolment of Students in Kurnool District from 2005-06 to 2011-12

		2005-06	2006-07	2007-08	2008-09	2009-10	2010-11	2011-12
Central Government	Boys	630	635	619	695	669	729	702
	Girls	469	444	471	528	490	497	494
State Government	Boys	15627	15205	15235	16341	16742	16216	15811
	Girls	15295	16283	16439	18583	19883	20471	22852
MPP-ZPP	Boys	196688	197678	193141	184173	179854	176723	180732
	Girls	180207	183804	183966	181053	179099	177132	181463
Municipal	Boys	13110	12138	11490	11576	10383	10329	10697
	Girls	14770	13903	13537	13345	12219	11854	11993
Private-Aided	Boys	25997	25327	24561	22747	20756	18793	17115
	Girls	24742	24840	24567	23327	21632	19708	18474
Private-Unaided	Boys	100137	116905	121206	129513	125750	130734	136271
	Girls	67093	79217	81459	86450	83873	88241	93172
Total	Boys	352189	367888	366252	365045	354154	353524	361328
	Girls	302576	318491	320439	323286	317196	317903	328448
	Total	654765	686379	686691	688331	671350	671427	689776

Source: 1.Commissioner and Director of School Education, State Project Director RVM (SSA)
2. District Educational Office, Kurnool

in 2010-11. The percentage of girls was highest in 2007-08, i.e., 43.21 per cent of the total. With regard to educational institutions run by State Government, the enrolment gradually increased, except in 2011-12. It is pertinent to note that the girl students outnumbered the boys in all the years, except in 2005-06. The percentage of girls studying in State Government schools also gradually increased and reached the highest of 59.11 per cent in 2011-12.

It is important to note that the enrolment in the MPP/ZPP managed schools gradually declined from 2007-08 to 2010-11. The number of girls enrolled in the MPP/ZPP managed schools was higher than that of the boys in all the years. In 2007-08 the percentage of girls to total enrolment in MPP/ZPP schools was highest at 54.09 per cent. In the case of Municipal schools, downward trend in enrolment is quite clear except during 2011-12. More than half of the enrolled students in Municipal schools were girls. The enrolment under private aided schools showed a gradual decline. In private aided schools, boys' strength was high during first two years and after that girls outnumbered the boys. The total enrolment under private unaided schools showed an upward trend except in 2009-10. It is very important to note that the percentage of girls in private unaided schools never crossed 41 per cent during 7 years. It means that the parents are sending girls to government schools and boys to private unaided schools. The percentage of girls in all the schools taken together ranged between 46.21 per cent and 47.62 per cent.

Stage-wise Enrolment

The stage-wise enrolment of students in Kurnool district from 2005-06 to 2011-12 is given in table 3.9. The data in table 3.10 shows that with regard to enrolment in classes I to V, the percentage of girls was about 48 per cent every year.

Table- 3.9
Stage-wise Enrolment of Students in Kurnool
District from 2005-06 to 2011-12

Year	Classes I-V		Classes - VI-VII		Classes -VIII-X		Classes - XI-XII		Classes - I-X		Classes - I-XII		
	Boys	Girls	Boys	Girls	Boys	Girls	Boys	Girls	Boys	Girls	Boys	Girls	Total
2005-06	202092	192423	65000	51724	72380	49070	69	41	339472	293217	352189	302576	654765
2006-07	205764	194871	66839	55057	74729	53249	66	30	347332	303177	367888	318491	686379
2007-08	200678	190482	68070	57462	76558	56557	60	33	345306	304501	366252	320439	686691
2008-09	198736	189860	66218	56726	79449	61861	59	44	344403	308447	365045	323286	688331
2009-10	197958	189148	65079	55784	80434	64559	66	41	343471	309491	354154	317196	671350
2010-11	200636	189259	64726	57252	78867	65208	217	193	344229	311719	353524	317903	671427
2011-12	206020	194363	66152	60934	78982	65921	73	211	351154	321218	361328	328448	689776

Source: 1.Commissioner and Director of School Education, State Project Director RVM (SSA)

2. District Educational Office, Kurnool

The enrolment of both boys and girls was highest at 205,764 and 194,871 respectively in 2006-07. With regard to enrolment in classes VI to VII, the percentage of girls gradually increased. In 2005-06 the percentage of girls enrolled in VI-VII classes was 44.31 per cent, which increased to 47.95 per cent by 2011-12. The total enrolment of students in classes VIII to X showed an upward trend during the first 5 years. In the same way, the enrolment of girls in classes VIII – X gradually increased during the above period. But the percentage of girls to total enrolment declined when compared to I - V classes and VI – VII classes. In case of Classes XI – XII, the percentage of girls further declined except in 2011-12. In classes XI to XII, the percentage of girls to total enrolment was as high as 74.30 per cent.

Management-wise Teachers

Table 3.10 shows the number of teachers working in schools under the management of different agencies. It may be seen that the percentage of women teachers never crossed 33.9 per cent in Central Government schools. The number of teachers working in State Government schools was not evenly distributed between men and women. The percentage of women teachers crossed 50 per cent mark in 2008-09 in State government schools. The total number of teachers in MPP/ZPP managed schools gradually increased, except in 2010-11. The percentage of women teachers in MPP/ZPP schools stood at 54 per cent of total in 2011-12. It is pertinent to note that the women teachers outnumbered men in Municipal schools in Kurnool district. The total number of teachers in private aided schools gradually declined, except in 2010-11. From 2008-09 onwards, the women teachers outnumbered men in private unaided schools in the district. The percentage of women teachers in private unaided schools stood at 52 per cent of total in 2011-12. The total teachers working under all the schools taken together stood at 20275 in 2011-12, comprising 11270 men (55.6%) and 9005 women (44.4%). Thus, on the whole, men outnumbered women in respect of teachers under all managements in Kurnool district.

Table – 3.10
Management wise working Teachers in Schools of Kurnool District

Year	Central Government		State Government		MPP-ZPP		Municipal		Private-Aided		Private-Unaided		Total		
	Men	Women	Men	Women	Men	Women	Men	Women	Men	Women	Men	Women	Men	Women	Total
2005-06	39	20	479	401	5405	3334	272	385	693	462	3290	2948	10178	7550	17728
2006-07	35	13	516	442	5538	3452	265	353	678	439	3547	3350	10579	8049	18628
2007-08	35	14	473	430	5423	3390	259	340	652	414	3477	3356	10319	7944	18263
2008-09	35	15	487	503	5615	3502	245	321	611	367	3383	3450	10376	8158	18534
2009-10	33	15	523	501	6046	3822	250	320	578	341	3292	3398	10722	8397	19119
2010-11	32	11	532	459	5956	3831	250	325	580	355	3704	3884	11054	8865	19919
2011-12	35	11	532	433	6627	4366	314	368	499	287	3263	3540	11270	9005	20275

Source: 1.Commissioner and Director of School
Education, State Project Director RVM (SSA)
2. District Educational Office, Kurnool

The Gross Enrolment Ratios in Kurnool district from 2005-06 to 2011-12 across gender and different school age groups are presented in table 3.11.

Table – 3.11
Gross Enrolment Ratios of Students in Kurnool District

Year	Gross Enrolment Ratio 6-10 Years			Gross Enrolment Ratio 11-12 Years			Gross Enrolment Ratio 13-15 Years		
	Boys	Girls	Total	Boys	Girls	Total	Boys	Girls	Total
2005-06	127.16	127.99	127.57	89.77	73.46	81.73	58.16	41.61	50.11
2006-07	114.82	113.95	114.39	85.68	74.37	80.17	62.38	47.3	55.07
2007-08	113.74	113.24	113.5	89.58	79.49	84.66	65.11	51.02	58.27
2008-09	114.4	114.76	114.57	89.46	80.36	85.02	68.85	56.67	62.93
2009-10	115.75	116.23	115.98	90.26	80.92	85.7	71.01	60.07	65.69
2010-11	119.14	118.24	118.70	92.16	85.05	88.39	70.94	61.62	66.40
2011-12	123.67	122.87	123.28	95.88	92.18	94.07	72.35	63.36	67.96

Source: 1.Commissioner and Director of School
Education, State Project Director RVM (SSA)
2. District Educational Office, Kurnool

It may be noted from table 3.11 that the Gross Enrolment Ratio (GER) of boys and girls declined with an increase in the age group. For instance, the gross enrolment of boys and girls of 6-10 years is 127.16 and 127.99 in 2005-06 respectively, whereas the corresponding figures stood at 58.16 and 41.61 for 13 to 15 years age group. Similarly, the gross enrolment of boys and girls of 6-10 years is 123.67 and 122.87 in 2011-12 respectively, while the corresponding figures stood at 72.35 and 63.36 for 13 to 15 years age group. The GER increased for both boys and girls in the age group of 11-12 years from 89.77 and 73.46 respectively in 2005-06 to 95.88 and 80.92 respectively in 2011-12. Similarly, the GER increased for both boys and girls in the age group of 13-15 years from 58.16 and 41.61 respectively in 2005-06 to 72.35 and 63.36 respectively in 2011-12. Thus, it could be inferred that the girls are lagging behind boys in respect of GER in all the age groups in 2011-12, more so in the age group of 13-15 years.

Dropout Rates at different stages of schooling

Table 3.13 shows the dropout rates of students in Kurnool district from 2005-06 to 2011-12 at different stages of schooling.

Table – 3.12
Dropout Rate of Students in Kurnool District

Year	I-V			I-VII			I-X		
	Boys	Girls	Total	Boys	Girls	Total	Boys	Girls	Total
2005-06	27.62	31.3	29.44	53.39	61.56	57.38	67.26	75.97	71.33
2006-07	27.42	33.86	30.63	48.95	58.37	53.6	66.44	73.96	69.99
2007-08	17.18	22.94	20.02	39.12	48.13	43.58	65.7	73.97	69.68
2008-09	16.93	22.39	19.63	39.2	48.08	43.63	63.13	70.9	66.92
2009-10	15.19	17.28	16.21	29.03	37.68	33.3	59.27	67.87	63.52
2010-11	19.10	22.15	20.60	28.92	36.83	32.83	53.42	61.54	57.44
2011-12	12.98	15.64	14.28	25.26	29.86	27.52	53.56	62.11	57.83

Source: 1.Commissioner and Director of School
Education, State Project Director RVM (SSA)
2. District Educational Office, Kurnool

It is heartening to note from table 3.12 that the dropout rate of students in Kurnool district gradually declined with varying degrees both in case of boys and girls. However, the dropout rate of both boys and girls increased with an increase in the grade/ class. The total dropout rate of students in classes I to V declined from 29.44 in 2005-06 to 14.28 in 2011-12, being higher in the case of boys than girls. More or less the same trends are visible in case of other two stages of classes, i.e., I-VII and I-X. The dropout rates were still high in class I-X both for boys and girls at 53.42 and 61.54 respectively in 2011-12. The girls seem to be in a disadvantageous position compared to boys in respect of class I-X.

PROGRESS OF NATIONAL CHILD LABOUR PROJECT

The National Child Labour Project has been implemented in Kurnool district since 1995-96. Table 3.13 shows the details of the number of centres established, number of children enrolled in bridge courses and the number of children mainstreamed since inception of NCLP in Kurnool district. It may be noted that on the whole, 52144 children were enrolled in bridge courses out of which 28698 children (55%) were mainstreamed into the formal schooling system. The performance in terms of the number of children enrolled and the number of children mainstreamed reached its peak during the period between 2001-02 and 2007-08. Thereafter, the number of centres decreased and the number of children enrolled and the number of children mainstreamed also showed a declining trend, but in terms of the percentage of mainstreamed children to enrolled children, the performance was at its best (90%) during 2011-12, while it varied between 31.6 per cent and 79.1 per cent during other years from 2008-09 to 2013-14.

The process followed under NCLP includes conducting micro level survey to identify the out-of-school children and formulate strategies to enrol them into bridge courses and later mainstream them into formal schooling system by admitting them in age-appropriate classes in the government schools.

Table 3.13
Number of Centres, Number of children enrolled and Number of children mainstreamed under National Child Labour Project in Kurnool District from 1995-96 to 2013-14

S. No.	Year	No of Centres	Number of Children enrolled	Number of children mainstreamed	% of enrolled children mainstreamed
1	1995-96	37	1850	11	0.59
2	1996-97	63	3150	407	12.9
3	1997-98	68	3400	820	24.1
4	1998-99	48	2400	1427	59.4
5	1999-00	93	4650	1610	34.6
6	2000-01	93	4650	1771	38.0
7	2001-02	93	4650	3103	66.7
8	2002-03	93	4650	4027	86.6
9	2003-04	93	4650	3634	78.1
10	2004-05	93	4650	2355	50.6
11	2005-06	93	4650	2255	48.4
12	2006-07	87	4201	3734	88.8
13	2007-08	36	1487	1256	84.4
14	2008-09	09	450	310	68.8
15	2009-10	18	1200	950	79.1
16	2010-11	09	436	328	75.2
17	2011-12	09	450	405	90.0
18	2012-13	09	260	130	50.0
19	2013-14	09	300	95	31.6
		Total	52144	28698	55.04

Source: 1.Commissioner and Director of School
          Education, State Project Director RVM (SSA)
          2. District Educational Office, Kurnool

Reasons for Children to be Out of School

Table 3.14 shows the reasons identified in the micro level surveys for the children to be out of school during 2004-05, 2005-06 and 2009-10. It may be noted that household work appears to be the prime reason for the children to be out of school during all the three years; the percentage of children reporting this reason varied between 49.9 per cent in 2005-06 and 38.4 per cent in 2009-10. Migration and earning compulsion also forced the children to be out of school; the percentage of children reporting migration as the main reason varied between 10 per cent in 2005-06 and 26.9 per cent in 2009-10, while the percentage of children reporting earning compulsion as the main reason varied between 6.2 per cent in 2005-06 and 26 per cent in 2009-10. The other reasons that forced the children to be out of school include lack of interest, failure in exam and socio-cultural reasons. Thus, earning compulsion and migration were the prime reasons for the children to be out of school in 2009-10 as against household work in 2004-05 and 2005-06. This indicates growing poverty and marginalization over time among the households comprising out-of-school children.

Table 3.14
Reasons for Children to be Out of School in Kurnool District

S.No.	Reasons for Children to be Out of School	2004-05		2005-06		2009-10	
		Number	% to Total	Number	% to Total	Number	% to Total
1	Lack of Interest	4430	10.0	3795	12.7	0	0
2	Household Work	17721	40.0	14945	49.9	2934	38.4
3	Migration	8860	20.0	2989	10.0	2056	26.9
4	Earning Compulsion	6645	15.0	1868	6.2	1986	26.0
5	Failure in Exam	2215	5.0	5602	18.7	0	0
6	Socio Cultural Reason	4430	10.0	748	2.5	662	8.7
	Total	44301	100.0	29947	100.0	7638	100.00

Source: 1.Commissioner and Director of School
Education, State Project Director RVM (SSA)
2. District Educational Office, Kurnool

Enrolment Status of Children

Table 3.15 presents the enrolment status of children in the age group of 6-14 years in Kurnool district from 2004-05 to 2012-13. It could be seen that the percentage of OOS children to total child population in the age group of 6-14 years accounted for 7.63 per cent in 2004-05, and gradually declined to 1.22 per cent in 2009-10. It increased to 2.71 per cent in 2011-12, but declined to 2.17 per cent and 2012-13.

Table 3.15
Status of Enrolment of children in the age group of 6-14 years in Kurnool District from 2004-05 to 2012-13

S. No.	Year	Child Population (5 to 14 years)	Enrolment	Out-of-School Children (OOS)	% OOS to child pop.
1	2004-05	580493	536191	44302	7.63
2	2005-06	555335	517975	37360	6.73
3	2006-07	580493	553686	26807	4.62
4	2007-08	NA	NA	NA	NA
5	2008-09	NA	NA	NA	NA
6	2009-10	556441	548534	7907	1.42
7	2010-11	553484	546724	6760	1.22
8	2011-12	596097	579940	16157	2.71
9	2012-13	575276	562820	12456	2.17

Source: 1.Commissioner and Director of School
Education, State Project Director RVM (SSA)
2. District Educational Office, Kurnool

Note: NA = not available

Distribution of Out-of-School Children by Age

The distribution of Out-of-School (OOS) children by age group is presented in table 3.16. It may be noted that most of the OOS children belonged to the age group of 11-14 years, when compared to those in the age group of 8-11 years and 6-8 years. The number of OOS children increased with the age in the district in respect of both boys and girls, indicating that more number of children dropped out at the upper primary level than those at the primary level. On the whole, girls (57%) outnumbered boys (43%) both during 2006-07 and 2007-08 among the OOS children in the age group of 6-14 years.

Table 3.16
Distribution of Out-of-School Children by Age Group in Kurnool District during 2006-07 and 2007-08

S. No.	Age Group	2006-07			2007-08		
		Boys	Girls	Total	Boys	Girls	Total
1	6-8 years	2209	2889	5098	128	162	290
2	8-11 years	2963	4016	6979	773	1151	1924
3	11-14 years	4710	6321	11031	2124	2897	5021
4	Total	9882	13226	23108	7498	9828	17326

Source: 1.Commissioner and Director of School Education, State Project Director RVM (SSA)
2. District Educational Office, Kurnool

The distribution of Out-of-School children by age in Kurnool district in 2010-11 is shown in table 3.18. It may be noted that the percentage of OOS children to total child population was higher in the age group of 11-14 years (2.05%) when compared to the age group of 6-11 years (0.82%), the percentage for the age group of 6-14 years being 1.22 per cent. The percentage of OOS children to total children was higher in the case of girls and that of boys in the age group of 6-11 years and 11-14 years and also when the two age groups are taken together.

Table 3.17
Child Population, Enrolment in School and Out-of-School Children in Kurnool District: 2010-11

S. No	Age group and Gender	Child Population	Enrolment in school	Out of School children	% of OOS children to Child Population
1.	**6 – 11 years**				
	Boys	191528	190163	1365	0.71
	Girls	181040	179345	1695	0.93
	Total	372568	369508	3060	0.82
2.	**11 – 14 years**				
	Boys	95901	94346	1555	1.62
	Girls	85015	82870	2145	2.52
	Total	180916	177216	3700	2.05
3.	**6 – 14 years**				
	Boys	287429	284509	2920	1.02
	Girls	266055	262215	3840	1.44
	Total	553484	546724	6760	1.22

Source: 1.Commissioner and Director of School
Education, State Project Director RVM (SSA)
2. District Educational Office, Kurnool

Strategies Adopted for Mainstreaming

Table 3.18 presents the strategies adopted for mainstreaming of OOS children in Kurnool district during 2007-08 and 2009-10. It could be seen that the most important strategy adopted was enrolment in residential bridge courses (56.7%) in 2007-08, followed by enrolment in Madarsaa/ Maktab (study centre for Muslims) (32.8%) and enrolment in non-residential bridge courses (10.5%). In 2009-10, the most important strategy adopted for mainstreaming of OOS children was direct admission into schools (30.4%), followed by enrolment in non-residential bridge courses (24.9%) and enrolment in residential bridge courses (20.6%). Other strategies (alternative and innovative education centres) were adopted to mainstream about 13.5 per cent of OOS children in 2009-10. Thus, the strategies were designed based on the basic characteristics of the households in which the OOS children were identified and keeping in view the main reasons reported by them for being out of school.

Table 3.18

Strategies adopted for Mainstreaming Out-of-School Children in Kurnool District

S. No.	Strategy	2007-08		2009-10	
		Number	% to Total	Number	% to Total
1	Direct enrolment into schools	0	0	2403	30.4
2	Enrolment in Non-residential Bridge courses	1309	10.5	1968	24.9
3	Enrolment in Residential Bridge courses	7073	56.7	1630	20.6
4	Enrolment in Madarsaa/Maktab	4092	32.8	836	10.6
5	Others	0	0	1070	13.5
	Total	12474	100.0	7907	100.0

Source: 1.Commissioner and Director of School
Education, State Project Director RVM (SSA)
2. District Educational Office, Kurnool

Special training was envisaged as the main strategy for mainstreaming OOS children during 2011-12 and 2012-13, as shown in table 3.19. It could be noted that the special training was planned in 2012-13 taking into account the left over cases during 2011-12 also. It was envisaged that out of 5979 OOS children identified for special training, 3703 (62%) would be covered under residential mode of training, while the remaining under non-residential mode of training.

Table 3.19
Special Training for Mainstreaming Out of School
Children in Kurnool District:
2011-12 and 2012-13

S. No.	Particulars	Number
1	OOSC identified for special training in 2011-12	7391
2	OOSC provided special training in 2011-12	3691
3	OOSC mainstreamed in age-appropriate class in 2011-12	1788
4	OOSC identified previously and proposed to be covered during 2012-13	1903
5	OOSC identified for special training in 2012-13	4076
6	Total OOSC proposed for special training in 2012-13	5979
7	Mode of special training – Residential	3703
8	Mode of special training – Non-residential	2276

Source: 1.Commissioner and Director of School
Education, State Project Director RVM (SSA)
2. District Educational Office, Kurnool

Funds Received and Expenditure Incurred

Table 3.20 shows the funds received and expenditure incurred under NCLP in Kurnool district from 1995-96 to 2013-14. It may be noted that funds received and expenditure incurred were high during the period from 2000-01 to 2007-08. Thereafter, there was a gradual decline in the funds received and expenditure incurred under the NCLP. This decline could be attributed to a decline in the OOS children to the total children in the age group of 6-14 years, mainly due to intensive efforts launched under the NCLP and partly due to other socio-economic changes taking place in the district.

90

Table 3.20
Funds Received and Expenditure Incurred under the NCLP in Kurnool District from 1995-96 to 2013-14
(Rs.)

Year	Funds received	Expenditure	Balance Amount
1995 – 96	32,46,678	16,26,298	16,20,380
1996 – 97	41,64,288	40,74,552	89,736
1997 – 98	96,58,022	60,77,186	35,80,836
1998 – 99	41,43,692	40,75,145	68,547
1999 – 2000	94,00,652	89,27,172	4,73,480
2000 – 01	1,56,04,523	1,36,98,947	19,05,576
2001 – 02	1,95,48,397	1,72,18,028	23,30,369
2002 – 03	1,95,86,846	1,78,32,272	17,54,574
2003 – 04	1,94,98,042	1,91,92,870	3,05,172
2004 – 05	2,42,99,650	2,27,72,903	15,26,747
2005 – 06	2,55,44,526	2,09,61,078	45,83,448
2006 – 07	1,21,13,100	1,80,00,561	58,87,461
2007 – 08	1,18,36,100	25,25,417	93,10,683
2008 – 09	93,10,683	47,18,673	45,92,010
2009 – 10	45,92,010	14,20,061	31,71,949
2010 – 11	31,71,949	15,52,971	16,18,978
2011 – 12	16,18,978	16,13,862	5,116
2012 – 13	21,75,116	14,22,771	7,52,345
2013 – 14	7,52,345	7,51,083	1,262

Source: 1.Commissioner and Director of School
Education, State Project Director RVM (SSA)
2. District Educational Office, Kurnool

Impact of NCLP

Table 3.21 shows the gross enrolment rate (GER), net enrolment rate (NER) and dropout rate among children in the age group of 6-14 years in Kurnool district from 2006-07 to 2010-11, based on which the impact of NCLP could be assessed to some extent. It may be seen that the GER and NER increased in the age group of 6-11 years and 11-14 years from 2006-07 to 2010-11. The dropout rate declined from 30.63 per cent in 2006-07 to 10.26 per cent in 2010-11 in the age group of 6-11 years, while it declined from 39.76 per cent in 2006-07 to 18.68 per cent in 2010-11

91

in the age group of 11-14 years. Thus, increase in GER
and NER and decline in the dropout rate clearly indicate
the positive impact of NCLP on mainstreaming the OOS
children, who include mostly the school dropouts and
some never enrolled children.

Table 3.21
Gross Enrolment Rate, Net Enrolment Rate and Dropout Rate among Children in the age group of 6-11 and 11-14 years in Kurnool District

S. No	Age group (Years)	2006-07	2007-08	2008-09	2009-10	2010-11
1	**6-11 years**					
	Gross Enrolment rate	87.79	89.33	107.05	106.80	105.65
	Net Enrolment Rate	85.37	87.26	99.00	98.55	99.13
	Dropout Rate	30.63	22.86	19.50	21.59	10.26
2	**11-14 years**					
	Gross Enrolment rate	95.46	101.93	90.74	96.67	94.48
	Net Enrolment Rate	64.05	71.41	82.02	81.47	86.11
	Dropout Rate	39.76	16.44	20.09	19.23	18.68

Source: 1.Commissioner and Director of School
Education, State Project Director RVM (SSA)
2. District Educational Office, Kurnool

Table 3.22 shows the GER, NER and Transition
Rate among children at the primary and upper primary
levels in rural and urban areas across social groups and
gender in Kurnool district during 2011-12. It may be
noted that the GER, NER and Transition Rate have
shown significant improvement across all social

categories and gender groups both in rural and urban areas. There is near parity at the district level in respect of transition rate for all the children and SC children, but the ST and minority children are slightly lagging behind. Similar trends could be noticed in respect of GER and NER in primary and upper primary levels. But, the gender disparities still persist in respect of GER and NER, especially at the upper primary level across all social groups.

Table 3.22
Gross Enrolment Rate, Net Enrolment Rate and Transition Rate among children at Primary and Upper Primary levels by Location, Social Category and Gender in Kurnool District – 2011-12

S. No.	Loca tion	Social Categor y	Primary				Upper Primary				Transitio n rate
			GER		NER		GER		NER		
			B	G	B	G	B	G	B	G	
1	Ru ral	All	98.44	97.27	98.35	97.12	94.61	96.23	95.91	94.09	83.01
		SC	98.24	97.30	98.13	97.12	93.65	95.78	95.45	92.92	84.34
		ST	99.34	98.88	99.31	98.82	96.49	96.80	96.56	95.51	77.07
		Minority	99.57	99.00	99.55	98.95	99.54	100.17	100.19	99.51	74.26
2	Ur ba n	All	98.50	97.90	98.43	98.79	96.68	98.01	97.89	96.45	104.20
		SC	98.96	98.52	98.90	98.42	97.06	98.17	98.06	96.87	104.12
		ST	96.37	93.20	96.09	92.85	85.78	92.84	92.19	85.12	107.69
		Minority	99.13	99.06	98.09	99.02	93.53	92.85	92.34	93.19	85.86
3	To tal	All	98.45	97.42	98.37	97.28	95.25	96.77	96.51	94.83	88.39
		SC	98.40	97.55	98.30	97.40	94.63	96.40	96.14	94.09	88.39
		ST	98.57	97.57	98.49	97.44	93.46	95.23	94.83	92.60	84.96
		Minority	99.39	99.02	99.37	98.98	96.48	97.06	96.85	96.48	78.90

Source: 1.Commissioner and Director of School Education, State Project Director RVM (SSA)

2. District Educational Office, Kurnool

SUMMING UP

To sum up, it may be said that the integrated approach followed by the government of Andhra Pradesh to tackle the twin problems of school dropout and child labour yielded some positive results, as indicated by an increase in the educational facilities in terms of the number of schools, teachers and teacher-pupil ratios over time along with an increase in the GER and NER and a decline in the dropout rate. In Kurnool district the main reasons for the children to be out of school were found to be household work, earning compulsion and migration. Appropriate strategies were formulated for mainstreaming the OOS children in the district from time to time, which include enrolment in residential and non-residential bridge courses and later joining them in government schools, direct admission into government schools in age-appropriate class, and special trainings. The strategies followed under NCLP and SSA for mainstreaming the OOS children successful to an average extent; about 55 per cent of the children enrolled in bridge courses were mainstreamed between 1995-96 and 2013-14 at the overall level, but the success rate increased over time. Further, the efforts initiated led   to an increase in GER, NER and transition rate and a decline in the dropout rates over time in the age groups of 6-11 years and 11-14 years. Even though parity was brought about between the SCs and all children in respect of GER and NER both among the boys and girls, the STs and Minorities are still lagging behind. The gender disparities in terms of GER, NER and dropout rates reduced to a great extent at the primary level, but continued to persist at the upper primary level.

CHAPTER –IV
SOCIO-ECONOMIC PROFILE OF SAMPLE
CHILDREN OF AND HOUSEHOLDS
INTRODUCTION

The socio-economic profile of the sample children and households needs to be examined in order to understand the circumstances in which the school dropouts have grown up, the quality of their living standards, and the factors responsible for their dropping out from school. In this chapter, an attempt is made to analyse the socio-economic characteristics of the sample children and households in terms of religion, caste category, demographic characteristics, education status, schooling status of children, occupation status, working status of children, land owned, ownership of house, type of house, amenities in the house such as drinking water, electricity, and toilet facility, movable assets and indebtedness. The analysis is done on the basis of gender of the sample children with a view to understanding the differences between the households comprising male and female school dropouts.

COMPOSITION OF SAMPLE CHILDREN

The sample children chosen for the study stood at 240, out of which 105 were males (44%) and 135 females (56%). Thus, there was greater proportion of females than males among the sample Children. All the sample children were in the school-going age group of 6-14 years.

RELIGION OF SAMPLE CHILDREN

In Indian society, religion is one of main social considerations of an individual. The distribution of the sample children by religion is presented in table 4.1. It may be noted from table 4.1 that a vast majority (89%) of the sample children were Hindus, while the remaining 11 per cent Muslims. The percentage of Hindus was higher among the male children (91%) when compared to that of females (87%). Thus, there is not much difference between the male and female sample children in regard to religion being pursued by them.

Table 4.1
Distribution of Sample Children by Religion

S. No.	Religion	No. of Children		
		Male	Female	Total
1	Hindu	96	117	213
	%	91.4	86.6	88.7
2	Muslim	9	18	27
	%	8.6	13.3	11.3
	Total	105	135	240
	%	100.00	100.00	100.00

Source: Field Data

CASTE CATEGORY OF SAMPLE CHILDREN

In Indian society caste is an important parameter, which determines the social status and position of an individual, especially in rural areas. The political and economic empowerment of people largely depends on the caste to which they belong. The distribution of sample children by caste category is given in table 4.2. It could be seen from table 4.2 that a majority (51%) of the sample children belonged to Backward Classes (BCs), being higher in respect of female children (54%) when compared to males (48%). The Scheduled Castes (SCs) accounted for nearly 33 per cent of the sample children, being higher among males (37%) as compared to females (29%). After BCs and SCs, Muslim minorities take the next important place in the case of sample children; about 11 per cent of the sample children belonged to Muslims, being higher in respect of female children (13%) when compared to males (9%). About 3 per cent of the sample children belonged to Scheduled Tribes (STs), while the other castes (OCs) accounted for only 2 per cent of the sample children. Thus, a vast majority of the sample children belonged to weaker sections of the society in terms of social status. It follows from the above a greater proportion of SCs are found among the school dropouts as compared to the proportion of SCs in total population at the district level.

Table 4.2

Caste Category of Sample Children

Source: Field Data

S. No.	Caste Category	No. of Children		
		Male	Female	Total
1	Scheduled Castes (SCs)	38	40	78
	%	36.9	29.2	32.5
2	Scheduled Tribes (STs)	5	2	7
	%	4.8	1.5	2.9
3	Backward Classes (BCs)	50	73	123
	%	47.6	54.1	51.3
4	Muslim Minorities	9	18	27
	%	8.6	13.3	11.3
5	Other Castes (OCs)	3	2	5
	%	2.9	1.5	2.1
	Total	105	135	240
	%	100.0	100.0	100.0

DEMOGRAPHIC CHARACTERISTICS OF SAMPLE CHILDREN HOUSEHOLDS

The households to which the sample children belonged were referred to as the sample children households. The demographic characteristics of the sample children households such as sex composition, household size, age group, marital status, etc., are examined here under.

Sex Composition

The sample children households comprised 1207 persons, out of which there were 573 males (47.5%) and 634 females (52.5%). The sex ratio (number of females

97

per 1000 males) worked out to 1106, which is very high when compared to the district average of 988 according to 2011 Census.

Household Size

The average household size of the sample children households worked out to 5.0, which is higher as compared to the district average of about 4.5. Thus, it may be inferred that the households comprising school dropouts had a higher sex ratio and household size, when compared to general population.

Distribution by Age Group

The distribution of members in the sample children households by age group is presented in table 4.3. It may be noted that the children in the school-going age group (6-14 years) accounted for 45 per cent of the total members in the sample children households, comprising a greater proportion of females (47%) as compared to males (43%). The percentage of children aged 14 years and below comprised about 47 per cent of total members in the sample children households, which looks on the high side when compared to that of general population. Persons belonging to the age group of 25-44 years accounted for about 31 per cent of total members in sample children households, comprising more females (33%) than males (28%). About 13 per cent of members in the sample children households belonged to the age group of 15-24 years. The percentage of members aged 60 years and above formed 1.4 per cent of the total in the case of sample children households. On the whole, the percentage of members belonging to economically productive age group of 15 – 59 years stood at about 52 per cent of the total members in the sample children households.

Table - 4.3
Distribution of Members in the Sample Households
by Age Group
Source: Field Data

S. No.	Age group (Years)		No. of members		
			Male	Female	Total
1	0 – 5		13	11	24
		%	2.3	1.7	2.0
2	6 – 14		246	296	542
		%	42.9	46.7	44.9
3	15 – 24		81	80	161
		%	14.1	12.6	13.3
4	25 – 44		161	209	370
		%	28.1	33.0	30.7
5	45 – 59		63	30	93
		%	11.0	4.7	7.7
6	60 +		9	8	17
		%	1.6	1.3	1.4
	Total		**573**	**634**	**1207**
		%	**100.0**	**100.0**	**100.0**

Marital Status

In the Indian society the marital status of a man/woman decides his/ her social and economic role in the society. The family obligation drives the people to search for higher incomes or supplementary incomes. Table 4.4 presents the marital status of members in the sample children households. It is evident from table 4.4 that most of the members in sample children households were unmarried. About 59 per cent of females and 58 per cent of males in the sample households were not married. About 41 per cent of the members in sample households are married with a

99

living partner. Among the married, the males slightly outnumbered females. Those who were widowed or separated constituted less than 1 per cent of members in the sample households.

Table 4. 4

Marital Status of Members in the Sample Households

S. No.	Marital Status		No. of members		
			Male	Female	Total
1	Unmarried		334	374	708
		%	58.3	59.0	58.7
2	Married		238	256	494
		%	41.5	40.4	40.9
3	Widowed		0	4	4
		%	0.0	0.6	0.3
4	Separated		1	0	1
		%	0.2	0.0	0.1
	Total		573	634	1207
		%	100.0	100.0	100.0

Source: Field Data

EDUCATION STATUS

Generally, education plays crucial role in taking rational decisions on all social and economic issues. The educated parents and family members are expected to understand better the importance of education to the children as compared to the uneducated. The education status of members, aged 7 years and above, in the sample children households is presented in table 4.5.

Table 4.5
Education Status of Members in the Sample
Households (7 years and above)

S. No.	Education Status		Male	Female	Total
			Male	**Female**	**Total**
1	Illiterate		271	364	635
		%	48.9	59.8	54.6
2	Just Literate		6	2	8
		%	1.1	0.3	0.7
2	Primary (1-5)		213	212	425
		%	38.4	34.8	36.5
3	Upper Primary (6-8)		30	17	47
		%	5.4	2.8	4.0
4	High school (9-10)		22	10	32
		%	4.0	1.6	2.8
5	Technical and College		12	4	16
		%	2.2	0.7	1.4
	Total		**554**	**609**	**1163**
		%	**100.0**	**100.0**	**100.00**

Source: Field Data

It is clear from table 4.5 that the educational status of members in sample children households is at the lowest level. Illiteracy levels were very high among both males and females at 49 per cent and 60 per cent, respectively, the average for all the members being 55 per cent. Only about 4 per cent of members in the sample households had education at upper primary level. Only about 3 per cent of members in the sample households had High School education, and just 1.4 had technical/ college education. As such, the educational levels of members in the sample households could be considered poor.

The literacy rate of 45 per cent for all members in the sample households could be considered very low when viewed against the district average of 60 per cent as per 2011 Census. Likewise, the male and female literacy rates of 51 per cent and 40 per cent, respectively, could be considered very low as compared to the district averages of 70 per cent and 50 per cent, respectively, according to 2011 Census. Thus, it may be said that the literacy levels and educational status of members in the sample households were low compared to overall picture at the district and state level. It follows from the above that high levels of illiteracy and low levels of educational status among the members of the sample households could be one major factor responsible for the school dropout problem.

OCCUPATION STATUS

The income of a household largely depends upon the nature of occupation pursued by its members. Occupation can be in any sector, organized or unorganized. Compared to unorganized sector, organized sector involves less physical strain and more leisure. The wage difference is also high between these two sectors. Hence, it is important to examine the occupation status of members in the sample households to ascertain the sustainability of income sources. The occupational status of members in the sample households is given table 4.6.

Table 4.6
Distribution of Members in the Sample Households
by Primary Occupation

S. No.	Primary Occupation	No. of Members		
		Male	Female	Total
1	Agricultural Labour	166	242	408
	%	29.0	38.2	33.8
2	Non-Agricultural Labour	129	173	302
	%	22.5	27.2	25.0
3	Cultivator	76	34	110
	%	13.3	5.4	9.1
4	Small Business	2	2	4
	%	0.3	0.3	0.3
5	Salaried	5	1	6
	%	0.9	0.2	0.5
4	Cannot Work	20	24	31
	%	2.5	3.8	2.6
5	Student	175	158	334
	%	30.5	24.9	27.7
	Total	573	634	1207
	%	100.0	100.0	100.0

Source: Field Data

Table 4.6 shows that about 34 per cent of members in the sample households were engaged in agricultural labour as their primary occupation. About 25 per cent of members in the sample households were dependent on non-agricultural labour as their primary occupation. The percentage of females was higher than that of males among those pursuing agricultural labour and non-agricultural labour as their main occupation. It means that in the study area female members contributing a lot for the economic wellbeing of the family. Only about 9 per cent of members in the sample households were dependent on cultivation as their main occupation. The percentage of members pursuing small business and salaried jobs together constituted just 1 per cent of the total members in the sample households. The students accounted for about 28 per cent of the total members in the sample households, being higher in the case of males when compared to females. The remaining members cannot work (2.6%).

Thus, it becomes clear that a large majority of the workers were dependent on wage labour – either agricultural labour or non-agricultural labour, and therefore are in a highly vulnerable situation because the availability of wage labour is uncertain. Thus, the sample households are deprived of sustainable sources of income, which could be one major reason for the existence of large number of out-of-school children on account of their inability to send them to school.

SCHOOLING STATUS OF CHILDREN

It is important to examine the schooling status of children in the school-going age group of 6-14 years in order to assess whether all the children in this age group were going to school or not. The schooling status of children in the age group of 6-14 years in the sample children households is presented in table 4.7.

Table -4. 7
Schooling status of Children (6-14 years) in the
Sample Households

S. No.	Schooling Status	No. of Children		
		Male	Female	Total
1	In School	167	150	317
	%	67.9	50.6	58.5
2	Dropout	38	71	109
	%	15.4	24.0	20.1
3	Never Enrolled	41	75	116
	%	16.6	25.3	21.4
	Total	246	296	542
	%	100.0	100.0	100.0

It may be noted from table 4.7 that only about 68 per cent male children and 51 per cent of female children aged 6-14 years in the sample households were going to school at the time of field survey, the average for all the children being 59 per cent. The dropout children accounted for 20 per cent of total children in the school-going age group, while the never enrolled children constituted 21 per cent. In the case of dropout children, females (24%) outnumbered males (15%). Similarly, the percentage of females (25%) was higher than that of males (17%) even among the never enrolled children. Thus, the situation with regard to the out-of-school children is very grim in respect of the sample households.

Despite the fact that 240 children from the sample households (240) were covered under NCLP, there were still 109 dropout children and 116 never enrolled children in these households. The large-scale presence of out-of-school (OOS) children in respect of the sample households is a clear indication of high potential for child labour in the study area. It makes a mockery of the efforts made for mainstreaming the OOS children. Another cause of concern is the persisting gender inequalities in the schooling status of children in the sample households; in the study area, the parents seem to be giving priority to males when compared to females while sending children to school.

WORKING STATUS OF CHILDREN

It is also important to examine the working status of children in the school-going age group of 6-14 years to understand whether the OOS children are doing some work, and, if yes whether it is on full-time or part-time basis. Table 4.8 shows the working status of children in the sample households. It may be seen that the children not taking up any work constituted about 46 per cent of total children in the age group of 6 – 14 years in the sample households; it is these children who were going to school. The percentage of males was on the high side (55%) when compared to that of females (39%) among those who were not doing any work and going to school.

On the other hand, a majority of children (54%) in the school-going age group were doing some work or the other. It was found that about 41 per cent of children were taking up work on full-time basis, while the remaining 13 per cent were undertaking part-time work, mostly in the agricultural sector. Those who were taking up full-time work were engaged in agricultural and non-agricultural labour and other stray jobs. The percentage of females was higher (49%) than that of males (32%) among those children taking up work on full-time basis. Thus, gender disparities are evident in the matter of taking up work by the school-going aged children in the sample households.

Table -4. 8
Working status of Children (6-14 years) in the
Sample Households

S. No.	Working Status		No. of Children		
			Male	Female	Total
1	Full-time		78	146	224
		%	31.7	49.3	41.3
2	Part-time		32	36	68
		%	13.0	12.2	12.6
3	Not working		136	114	250
		%	55.3	38.5	46.1
	Total		246	296	542
		%	100.0	100.0	100.0

Source: Field Data

LAND OWNERSHIP

The economic status of a household depends on the land possessed, more so in in rural areas. As such, it is important to examine the land ownership status of sample households. Table 4.9 shows the land possessed by the sample children households.

Table 4. 9
Land Possessed by the Sample Children Households

S. No.	Land owned (acres)		No. of Households		
			Male	Female	Total
1	Nil		60	87	147
		%	57.1	64.4	61.3
2	1.0		9	13	22
		%	8.6	9.6	9.2
3	2.0		2	6	8
		%	1.9	4.4	3.3
4	3.0		10	7	17
		%	9.5	5.2	7.1
5	4.0		8	7	15

		%	7.6	5.2	6.3
6	5.0		16	15	31
		%	15.2	11.1	12.9
	Total		105	135	240
		%	100.0	100.0	100.0

Source: Field Data

It becomes clear from table 4.9 that a majority (61%) of the sample children households do not possess any agricultural land. Of those who possessed some agricultural land, most of them possessed agricultural land to the tune of 1-3 acres; about 20 per cent of the sample households belonged to this category. While 6 per cent of the sample households possessed 4 acres of land, those possessing 5 acres of land constituted 13 per cent of the total. None of the sample households possessed more than 5 acres of land. Thus, it may be inferred that over 60 per cent of the sample households were landless, and of the remaining, a majority of them possessed land to the tune of 3 acres or less. It is also important to note that although 39 per cent of the sample households possessed some land or the other, yet there were just 9 per cent members in the sample households pursuing cultivation as their main occupation. It follows from the above that the land owned by the sample households is rain-fed and unviable for cultivation, unable to generate income on a sustainable basis.

HOUSING SITUATION

The housing situation of the sample households indicates the quality of life of household members. Table 4.10 presents the housing situation in respect of the sample children households in terms of ownership of house, type of house and access to amenities such as electricity, safe drinking water and sanitation.

Ownership of House

It could be seen from table 4.10 that about 66 per cent of the sample households were residing in their own house, more so among the female children households (70%) when compared to male children households (60%). About 31 per cent of the sample households reported that they resided in government-given houses. Only about 3 per cent of the sample households lived in rented houses. Thus, as far as ownership of house is concerned, a majority of the sample households either lived in own houses or government-given houses.

Table 4.10

Housing Situation in respect of the Sample Children Households

S. No.	Particulars	No. of Households		
		Male (N=105)	Female (N=135)	Total (N=240)
1	**Status of House**			
	Government-given	36	39	75
	%	34.3	28.9	31.3
	Own house	63	95	158
	%	60.0	70.4	65.8
	Rented	6	1	7
	%	5.8	0.7	2.9
2	**Type of House**			
	Katcha	31	31	62
	%	29.5	23.0	25.8
	Pucca	47	57	104
	%	44.8	42.2	43.3
	Semi-Pucca	27	47	74
	%	25.7	34.8	30.8

3	Electricity Connection				
	Yes		88	123	211
		%	83.8	91.1	87.9
	No		17	12	29
		%	16.2	8.9	12.1
4	**Sanitation Facility**				
	Yes		8	6	14
		%	7.6	4.4	5.8
	No		97	129	226
		%	92.4	95.6	94.2
5	**Drinking Water Facility**				
	Public Bore well		12	8	20
		%	11.4	5.9	8.3
	Public Tap		93	127	220
		%	88.6	94.1	91.7
	Total		100.0	100.0	100.0

Source: Field Data

Type of House

The type of house in which a household lives denotes its economic status. If the sample children households are living in unsafe dwellings, their educational achievements may be adversely affected. The data in table 4.10 shows that about 43 per cent of sample children households lived in pucca houses and 31 per cent in semi-pucca houses. About 26 per cent of the sample households lived in Kachha houses or huts. Thus, only 43 per cent of the sample households resided in safe dwellings and the remaining 57 per cent either lived in semi-pucca or kachha houses.

Electricity Connection

It becomes evident from table 4.10 that a vast majority (88%) of the sample children households had the electricity connection in the study area; the corresponding figures for male and female children households stood at 84 per cent and 91 per cent, respectively. However, about 12 per cent of the sample children households had no electricity connection, being higher in respect of males (16%) as compared to females (9%). Thus, a vast majority of the sample households had electricity connection.

Sanitation Facility

A vast majority (94%) of the sample children households had no access to sanitation facility (individual toilet), as per the data presented in table 2.10. Only about 6 per cent of the sample children households had the individual toilet facility. Thus, the access to sanitation is very low among the sample households. This is despite the Total Sanitation Campaign launched in the country over a long time.

Source of Drinking Water

Table 4.10 shows that as many as 92 per cent of the sample children households depended on public tap as the main source of drinking water. The percentage of sample households depending on public tap as the main source of drinking water was slightly higher in the case of female children households (94%) when compared to male children households (89%). Nearly 8 per cent of the sample children households depended on public bore well as the main source of drinking water. Thus, the sample children households were deprived of safe drinking water facility.

POSSESSION OF MOVABLE ASSETS

Table 4.11 shows the possession of movable assets in the sample children households. It may be noted that the most of the households do not possess even the common assets such as electric fans and Television. Only 35 per cent of the sample households possessed the electric fans, while those possessing Television stood at just 24%; no substantial variations were found between the households comprising male and female sample children in this regard. Another important asset possessed by the sample households

111

was gas stove, more so among households comprising female dropouts than those comprising male dropouts. About 28 per cent of the households had access to gas stove, obtained by them under Deepam scheme of the Government of Andhra Pradesh. Another important asset possessed by the sample children households include motorbike (24%). Further, about 35 per cent of the sample households reported possession of silver ornaments to some extent, while those possessing gold ornaments to a very limited extent stood at 15 per cent. Only one per cent of the sample households possessed bicycle. Thus, it is clear the asset position of the sample households in respect of movable assets is poor.

Table 4.11
Possession of Movable Assets by the Sample Children Households

S. No	Name of the Assets		No. of Households Possessing		
			Male	Female	Total
1	Television		26	31	57
		%	24.8	23.0	23.7
2	Motorbike		21	30	51
		%	20.0	22.2	21.2
3	Bicycle		3	0	3
		%	2.9	0.0	1.2
4	Gold		22	15	37
		%	21.0	11.1	15.4
5	Silver		25	59	84
		%	23.8	43.7	35.0
6	Gas Stove		21	44	66
		%	20.0	32.6	27.5
7	Electric Fans		31	48	79
		%	29.5	35.5	32.9
	Total (N)		**105**	**135**	**240**

Source: Field Data

Table 4.12 shows distribution of sample households by the value of movable assets possessed. It may be seen from table 4.12 that about 17 per cent of the sample households did not possess any movable assets. The value of the household assets possessed by a majority (70%) of the sample households was only up to Rs.10000. Only about 11 per cent of the sample households possessed movable assets worth Rs.10000 – Rs.25000. Only about 1 per cent of the sample households possessed movable assets worth above Rs.25000. There were no substantial variations between the two categories of households comprising male and female sample children with regard to the value of movable assets possessed.

Table 4.12
Value of Movable Assets Possessed by the Sample Children Households

S. No.	Value of Movable Assets (Rs.)		No. of Households		
			Male	Female	Total
1	Nil		23	18	41
		%	21.9	13.3	17.1
2	Up to 10000		65	104	169
		%	61.9	77.6	70.4
3	10000 – 25000		15	11	26
		%	14.3	8.2	10.8
4	25000 – 50000		2	2	4
		%	1.9	1.5	1.7
	Total		105	135	240
		%	100.0	100.0	100.0

Source: Field Data

EXTENT OF INDEBTEDNESS

The educational opportunity of children in a particular household depends upon the economic position of that household. A household drowned in debts cannot afford to provide even the basic education of children. Instead of sending their children to school, the parents ask them to take up some work and earn something for the economic betterment of the family. Therefore, it becomes important to study the extent of indebtedness of the sample children households, as presented in table 4.13.

Table 4.13
Distribution of Sample Children Households by Outstanding Debt

S. No.	Outstanding debt (Rs.)	No. of Households		
		Male	Female	Total
1	Up to 25000	90	121	211
	%	85.7	89.6	87.9
2	25000-50000	14	12	26
	%	13.3	8.9	10.8
3	50000-75000	1	0	1
	%	1.0	0.0	0.4
4	75000-100000	0	2	2
	%	0.0	1.5	0.8
	Total	105	135	240
	%	100.0	100.0	100.0

Source: Field Data

It may be noted from table 4.13 that all the sample households had some amount of indebt. But a preponderant majority, i.e., 88 per cent, of the sample households had an outstanding debt of less than Rs.25 000. About 11 per cent of the sample households had an outstanding debt ranging from Rs.25000 to Rs.50000. Only one household had an outstanding debt in the range of Rs.50000 to Rs.75000, while two households had an outstanding debt in the range of Rs.75000 to Rs.100000. Thus, even though all the sample households were in debt, the amount of outstanding debt is less than Rs.25000 in most cases. Perhaps, the low levels of indebtedness among the sample households could be due to low asset position of the households in terms of house, land and movable assets.

SUMMING UP

To sum up, it may be said that most of the sample children pursued the Hindu religion and a majority of them belonged to weaker sections of the society in terms of both social and economic status. A majority of the sample children hailed from BCs, followed by SCs and Minorities. The demographic characteristics of the sample children households revealed that the sex ratio and household size were higher when compared to general population at the district level. The literacy rates were very low both among the males and females in the case of the sample households when viewed against the averages at the district and state level. Most of the members in the sample households had low levels of education, mostly confining to primary or upper primary level. Very few members had High School and College education. Most of the members were engaged as agricultural or non-agricultural labour, and a few as cultivators. The occupational diversification is very poor in respect of the sample children households; only a negligible proportion of members were pursuing small business or salaried jobs. It is matter of serious concern that there were a sizeable section of OOS children (41%) among the school-going age group of 6-14 years, and most of them were engaged in work on full-time or part-time basis. Thus, a large-scale presence of child labour in the sample households, despite the fact that one child from each of these households was covered under NCLP, makes a mockery of the Constitutional provisions relating to child labour and RTE Act, 2009.

A majority of the sample households were landless, and most of those who were in possession of land had 1-3 acres. About two-thirds of the sample households had own houses, while the remaining lived in government-given houses. Not even half of the sample households lived in pucca houses. Even though a vast majority of the households had access to electricity, their access to sanitation and safe drinking water was very much limited. The position of the sample households could be considered very poor in terms of amenities and movable assets. All the sample households were in debt, although the amount of outstanding debt was less than Rs.10000 per household. Thus, the socio-economic profile of the sample children and their households indicate that they hailed from a very poor social and economic background.

CHAPTER - V
MAINSTREAMING OF SCHOOL DROPOUTS IN
THE STUDY AREA: AN EMPERIAL ANALYSIS
INTRODUCTION

One of the main objectives of National Child Labour Projects (NCLP) was to identify the out-of-school (OOS) children and child labourers in the age group of 6 -14 years and mainstream them into the formal education system either directly admitting them in age-appropriate classes or through conduct residential or non-residential bridge courses at specified centres and later enrolling them into government schools. The OOS children mostly comprise the school dropouts and also a few never enrolled children. The NCLP was in operation since 1995-96 in the study district of Kurnool in Andhra Pradesh. The mainstreaming of school dropouts was taken up in the district under the NCLP in collaboration with Sarva Siksha Abhiyan (SSA) launched in 2000-01 aimed at universalizing the elementary education in the country. The sample children were chosen from among the OOS children who were enrolled into bridge courses during 2007-08 and 2008-09 with a view to admitting them into age-appropriate classes in government schools.

In this chapter, an attempt has been made to study the process of mainstreaming the sample children into formal education system, focusing on how they were enrolled into bridge courses, what was the nature of bridge courses, what facilities were provided at the bridge courses, into which schools they were admitted, and how they were feeling in the new schools, what is their opinion on the school environment, curriculum, teachers, facilities/ amenities available, etc. The analysis has been done by gender of the sample children, aimed to study the effectiveness with which the process of mainstreaming the school dropouts had taken place. Before studying the process of mainstreaming the sample children, it is important to

117

study the past history of sample children, which will help us in understanding the stage at which they dropped out, reasons for their dropping out, and what occupations they pursued before they were enrolled into bridge courses, in order to have a correct perspective of the problem.

PAST HISTORY OF SAMPLE CHILDREN

This analysis focuses on what the sample children were doing before joining the bridge courses.

Past Schooling Status

The past schooling status of sample children is presented in table 5.1. It may be noted that a vast majority (91%) of the sample children were school dropouts. It means that they have had access to formal education before dropping out of school. The percentage of school dropouts was higher among the males (94%) than that of females (88%). It follows that only about 9% of the sample children were never enrolled into school, meaning that they had no access to formal schooling system earlier. Among the never enrolled children, the females were in greater proportion (12%) when compared to males (6%). This indicates the discrimination shown towards girls in enrolling them into school in the study area. Thus, the parents had shown preference to boys in the matter of enrolling them into school. It also serves as a pointer to the fact that over 90 per cent of the OOS children were school dropouts and the rest never enrolled children and to the persisting gender inequalities in the enrolment of children into school.

Table 5.1
Past Schooling Status of Sample Children

S. No.	Schooling Status	No. of Children		
		Male	Female	Total
1	School dropout	99	119	218
	%	94.3	88.1	90.8
2	Never enrolled	6	16	22
	%	5.7	11.9	9.2
	Total	105	135	240
	%	100.0	100.0	100.0

Stage of Dropping out from School

The stage or class at which the sample children dropped out from school is presented in table 5.2.

Table 5.2
Stage of Dropping out from School in the case of Sample Children

S. No.	Stage/ Class	No. of Children		
		Male	Female	Total
1	Never enrolled	6	16	22
	%	5.7	11.9	9.2
2	3rd Class	4	13	17
	%	3.8	9.6	7.1
3	4th Class	32	30	62
	%	30.5	22.2	25.8
4	5th Class	33	41	74
	%	31.4	30.4	30.8
5	6th class	30	32	62
	%	28.6	23.7	25.8
6	7th Class	0	3	3
	%	0	2.2	1.3
	Total	105	135	240
	%	100.00	100.00	100.00

It is evident from table 5.2 that a considerable proportion of sample children (31%) discontinued from school in 5th Class. The important reasons for this phenomenon as observed by this researcher are given below:

1. The non-availability of upper primary and high schools in all the study villages after the children complete primary education.
2. The parents felt that their children acquired enough knowledge to read and write in mother tongue.

About 26 per cent of the sample children discontinued from school in 4th Class, while about 26 per cent had dropped out in 6th Class. About 7 per cent of the sample children dropped out in 3rd Class. On the whole, about 64 per cent of the sample children dropped out at Primary level, while about 27 per cent dropped out at the Upper Primary level. There were about 9 per cent of the sample children who were never enrolled into school. Further, no substantial differences were observed between males and females in regard to the stage at which the sample children dropped out from school, except in 3rd class where a greater proportion of females dropped out from school when compared to males.

Age of Dropping out from School

The interest or disinterest of children on education depends on the age of children. Age is an important factor for psychological deviation according to several psychologists. As such, it may of some use to study the age at which the sample children dropped out from school. Table 5.3 shows the age of dropping out from school in respect of the sample children.

120

Table-5.3
Age of Dropping out from School in respect of
Sample Children

S. No.	Age Group (years)	No. of Children		
		Male	Female	Total
1	6 – 8	11	13	24
	%	10.4	9.6	10.0
2	8 – 10	44	58	102
	%	41.9	42.9	42.5
3	10 – 13	50	64	114
	%	47.6	47.4	47.5
	Total	105	135	240
	%	100.0	100.0	100.0

As per table 5.3, about 47.5 per cent of the sample children dropped out from school after they had completed 10 years of age. In rural areas, parents assign different works to their children during the age group of 10 to 13 years. About 42.5 per cent of children dropped from school during the age group of 8 to 10 years. During the field survey it was observed that the children in the age group of 8 to 10 years, especially girls, were left at home to look after their younger siblings or cousins. About 10 per cent of children dropped from school in the age group of 6 to 8 years. On the whole, a majority (58%) of the sample children had dropped out from school even before they completed 10 years of age, while the rest had dropped out from school in the age group of 10 to 13 years.

Decision to drop out from school

The decision to drop out from school will be usually taken by parents or relatives or in some cases by the children themselves. Table 5.11 shows the distribution of sample children by who took the decision to drop out from school.

121

Table: 5.4
Decision to Drop out from School in the case of Sample Children

S. N o.	Decision to Drop out from school		No. of Children		
			Male	Fema le	Tota l
1	Own		38	42	80
		%	36.2	31.1	33.3
2	Parents		36	59	95
		%	34.3	43.7	39.6
3	Relatives		31	34	65
		%	29.5	25.2	27.1
	Total		105	135	240
		%	100. 00	100.0 0	100. 00

It is evident from table 5.4 that in case of about 40 per cent of the sample children, the parents took the decision to drop their children from school, the corresponding figure being higher among the girls (44%) when compared to boys (34%). About one-third of the sample children had taken the decision to drop out from school on their own, such a percentage being higher among the boys (36%) that that of girls (31%). It may also be seen that the relatives took the decision to drop the sample children out from school in respect of 27 per cent, such a percentage being higher in the case of boys (30%) as compared to girls (25%). On the whole, it is clear that either the parents or the relatives took the decision and were instrumental in dropping out the sample children from school in respect of two-thirds of sample children, while about one-third of the sample children took such a decision on their own, perhaps influenced by their friends or seniors in the school who had dropped out from school earlier.

Reasons for Dropping out from School

Considerable research has been underway to define the characteristics of dropouts and to develop tools to identify children "at risk" of dropping out of school. It has been repeatedly observed that low-achievers and students from low socio-economic backgrounds are at much higher risk of dropping out, which could be due to several reasons such as inadequate parenting, inability to afford the educational expenditure, poor schooling infrastructure, de-motivated teachers, pressure to augment family income, accompanied by a view that schooling has limited economic returns; peers with low aspirations; poor nutrition and health; and too few role models in the community. For policy makers to develop effective interventions, it is essential to ascertain which factors are most important for identifying school leavers, as dropouts are not a homogenous group, but early warning signs can help identify those most at risk and suitable strategies could be evolved for them.

One of the key problems is that students do not usually drop out for a single reason. Multiple factors are at play and no single risk factor can accurately predict who will dropout and why. Three sets of factors, viz., household, school and child related, primarily contribute to the phenomenon of dropping out from school. At the same time it is important to borne in mind that these three sets of factors do not influence dropping out from school independently but intertwined with each other producing a net effect of dropout. As an illustration one can argue that academic inability to cope with academic rigor and inability to bear the expenditure on private tuition interact and lead to dropout.

The parents reported that the most vital factor responsible for dropping out their children from school is their inability to meet the cost of schooling. During the field survey, the children and their parents talked

123

about difficulties in paying for school fees and other school related expenses, especially when the main bread-earner (father) was without a job or somebody fell sick in the family.

Table 5.5 presents the reasons for dropping out from school from the perspective of the parents of the sample children. It could be noted that the main reason for dropping out the sample children was the financial constraints, as stated by 45 per cent of the sample respondents. About 23 per cent of the sample respondents reported household factors as the main reason for dropping out their children from school. While 18 per cent of the sample respondents reported school factors as the main reason for dropping out their children from school, about 14 per cent reported individual or child related factors as the main reason. There were no substantial differences between the households comprising male and female dropouts with regard to main reasons for dropping out children from school. These reasons are further analysed in detail here.

Table 5.5
Main Reasons for dropping out from school in the case of sample children

S. No.	Reasons for Dropping out from school		No. of Children		
			Male	Female	Total
1	Financial Constraints		50	59	109
		%	47.6	43.7	45.4
2	Household Factors		22	33	55
		%	21.0	24.4	22.9
3	School factors		20	23	43
		%	19.0	17.0	17.9
4	Individual or Child Factors		13	20	33
		%	12.4	14.8	13.8
	Total		105	135	240
		%	100	100	100

Financial Constraints

Educational expenditure is on two counts, namely public and private. The expenditure incurred by the State in providing infrastructural arrangements for education, like creating facilities in the form of building and maintenance of schools, provision of teachers, payment of teacher salary, and other planned and non-planned grants are a part of the public expenditure. Private expenditure on education refers to the expenditure incurred by the parents and households. This is mainly incurred towards the payment of fees, private tuition, stationery, uniform, transport, etc. A number of studies highlight the linkage between poverty and dropping out from the school. A few research studies indicate that the cost of schooling, including fees, is one of the main reasons for dropping out from school. About 45.4 per cent of the sample respondents reported that the most significant factor for dropping out their children from school was their inability to meet the cost of schooling.

Household Factors

Socio-economic and cultural background of the households is also one of the most significant contributors to the continuation or discontinuation of the child in school. Poverty of the parents still remains one of the significant causes for the low participation of children in schooling. About 22.9 per cent of the sample respondents reported household factors as mainly responsible for dropping out their children from schools.

School factors

It is widely acknowledged that infrastructural facilities, school environment, and teachers' attitude exert powerful influences on student's interest or disinterest in studies including dropout rates. In this context, the PROBE team (1999) and Balgopalan and Subramanian (2003) describe discrimination against socially disadvantaged groups as terrible and exclusionary. They reported that children from the upper classes are joining private schools and the poor are basically attending government schools with some belonging to the Scheduled Caste and Scheduled Tribe groups and teachers belonging to the so-called upper castes. Consequently, the attitude of the teachers, disinterest in teaching these disadvantaged children and poor infrastructural facilities like unavailability of functional toilets, improper seating arrangements, etc., are found to be some of the important reasons for pushing out the children from school. Findings from the field survey also confirm some of these observations, as about 18 per cent of the sample respondents reported school related factors as the main reason for dropping out their children from school. It was observed, however, that the infrastructural facilities in schools in the study areas appear to be fairly good, even though improvement here and there is very much necessary. The schools had pucca or semi-pucca buildings, but amenities such as desks, computers, safe drinking water, and functional toilets were found wanting in most cases.

Individual or Child Factors

The child related factors are closely associated with the family and school related factors. Financial constraints and inappropriate school environment tend to de-motivate the children, making them lose interest in their studies and thus leading to their eventual dropping out from school. Further, household circumstances and academic failure increased students' alienation from school, leading to absenteeism, which also influenced their dropping out from school.

As the children living in rural and slum areas do not have favourable academic environment at home, and even in school the teachers lack motivation to teach, due to which the incidence of failure is very high among them. It was found that about 14 per cent of the sample respondents cited failure as the most significant reason for dropping out their children from school, as detention in the same grade caused embarrassment to the children. Further, it was reported that even after repeating the same grade they could not understand the subject matter and as such started loosing interest in studies. Thus, most of the students who failed had difficulty in understanding all the subjects; especially, they found Maths, Science and English very difficult.

It has often been observed that poor understanding at the elementary level is the main factor contributing to low comprehension at the secondary level. Researchers also reported connection between measures of academic performance in early elementary school and dropout behaviour before high school graduation. They emphasized the need for examining the causes of dropout before high school, as many students were observed to be dropping out before Grade X. Those who reach secondary level with weak academic understanding find it difficult to sustain.

Occupation of Sample Children before joining Bridge Courses

It is unethical as well as unlawful to engage children in works, especially when they are aged 14 years or less. Before joining bridge courses, the sample children reported that they had taken up different types of work after dropping out from school. As such, they were asked to give the particulars about the works they had undertaken in the time period after dropping out from school and before joining bridge courses. The types of work undertaken by sample children before joining bridge courses are presented in table 5.6. It may be seen from table 5.6 that the sample children had taken up 5 types of work before their admission into bridge courses. Among 5 types of work, about 31 per cent of sample children were engaged in stone breaking (stone chips) work. Construction related works were undertaken by about 23 per cent of sample children. About 22 per cent of the sample children were engaged as agricultural labour. Sheep rearing was another important work taken up by about 9 per cent of the sample children. There were also about 5 per cent of sample children worked in auto garages. On the whole, about 89 per cent of the sample children had taken up some work or other, after dropping out from school and before joining bridge courses, and there were no substantial variations between the two categories of households in this regard. The remaining 11 per cent of sample children had not taken up any work, after dropping out from school and before joining bridge courses.

Table 5.6
Occupation of the Sample Children before joining Bridge Courses

S. No.	Occupation	No. of Children		
		Male	Female	Total
1	Construction Work	23	31	54
	%	22.3	22.6	22.5
2	Stone breaking	29	45	74
	%	28.2	32.8	30.8
3	Agricultural labour	23	29	52
	%	22.3	21.2	21.7
4	Auto garage	3	10	13
	%	2.9	7.3	5.4
5	Sheep rearing	13	8	21
	%	12.6	5.8	8.8
6	No Work	12	14	26
	%	11.7	10.2	10.8
	Total	103	137	240
	%	100.0	100.0	100.0

Age at the time of taking up work

As per the provisions of the Indian Constitution, children below the age of 14 years shall not be employed in any work or industry. As such, it would be important to study the age at which the sample children started taking up work for the first time.

Table 5.7

Age at the time of taking up work for the first time in the case of Sample Children

S. No.	Age (years)	No of Sample Children		
		Male	Female	Total
1	9	13	19	32
	%	12.4	14.1	13.3
2	10	64	80	144
	%	61.0	59.3	60
3	11	14	19	33
	%	13.3	14.1	13.8
4	12	2	3	5
	%	1.9	2.2	2.1
5	No Work	12	14	26
	%	11.4	10.4	10.8
	Total	105	135	240
	%	100.0	100.0	100.0

Table 5.7 shows the age of the sample children when they took up work for the first time. It could be seen from table 5.7 that a majority (60%) of sample children took up work for the first time at the age of 10 years. It may also be seen that the sample children who had taken up work for the first time at the age of 9 years age constituted about 13 per cent of the total. Thus, nearly three-fourths of the sample children took up work for the first time at a tender age of 9 or 10 years. There were about 14 per cent of the sample

children who took up work at the age of 11 years, while about 2 per cent started working at the age of 12 years. On the whole, 89 per cent of the sample children were engaged in different works when they were aged between 9 and 12 years. There were only 11 per cent of the sample children who did not take up any work after they had dropped out from school and before joining the bridge courses.

Illness while Performing Economic Activity

When the children were engaged in different kinds of works, it is likely that they might have faced illnesses. Therefore it would be important to study the kinds of illnesses experienced by the sample children while they undertook economic activities. A question was asked to the sample children whether they suffered any illnesses before joining the bridge courses and, if yes, what kinds of illnesses they suffered. Table 5.8 shows the illness while performing economic activity in the case of sample children. It may be seen that a preponderant majority (90%) of sample children suffered due to illness while performing economic activities before joining bridge courses. These might have also included some children who had not taken up any work at that time. It was found that a slightly higher proportion of female children (92%) suffered due to illness than the male children (88%). This could be due to the fact that female children are more malnourished when compared to male children and have less resistance to diseases. Only 10 per cent of sample children reported that they never suffered from any illnesses while performing economic activities.

Table 5.8
Illness while Performing Economic Activity in the case of Sample Children

S. N o	Illness while Performing Economic Activity	No. of Children		
		Male	Femal e	Total
1	Yes	92	124	216
	%	87.6	91.9	90.0
2	No	13	11	24
	%	12.4	8.1	10.0
	Total	105	135	240
	%	100.00	100.00	100.00

Kinds of illness suffered while Working

The sample children, who reported that they experienced illness while working, were further asked with regard to the kinds of illnesses they suffered from. The kinds of illnesses suffered by the sample children while working are presented in table 5.9. It is evident from table 5.9 that nearly 38 per cent of sample children suffered from chickun gunya. It was found that a higher proportion of girls (40%) suffered from chickun gunya than that of boys (35%). About 33 per cent of sample children suffered from Malaria, such a percentage being higher among the girls (35%) than that of boys (31%). The diseases like Dengue, Pneumonia, Diarrhoea, Chicken pox, etc., were the other illnesses suffered by about 19 per cent of the sample children, such a percentage being higher among the boys (22%) than that of girls (17%). About 10 per cent of sample children were free from any illness. Thus, most of the sample children suffered from chickun gunya, malaria and other diseases while working.

131

Table 5.9
Kinds of Illness suffered by Sample Children while Working

S. No.	Kind of Illness		No. of Children		
			Male	Female	Total
1	Malaria		32	47	79
		%	30.5	34.8	32.9
2	Chickun Gunya		37	54	91
		%	35.2	40.0	37.9
3	Other Diseases		23	23	46
		%	21.9	17.1	19.2
4	No Illness		13	11	24
		%	12.4	8.1	10.0
	Total		105	135	240
		%	100.0	100.0	100.0

Consultation of Doctor

Consultation of qualified doctor is essential for early curing of diseases. Therefore, it is important to ascertain whether the sample children consulted doctor when they suffered from illnesses while working, and if yes, whether the doctors were qualified. The sample children were asked to give particulars on whether they consulted doctor after falling ill. Table 5.10 shows the particulars on consultation of doctor in the case of sample children when they suffered from illness while working. It is clear from table 5.10 that all those sample children who reported some kind of illness while working consulted the doctor.

132

Table: 5.10
Consultation with Doctor in times of Illness while working in the case of Sample Children

S. No.	Whether Consulted Doctor?	No. of Children		
		Male	Female	Total
1	Yes	92	124	216
	%	87.6	91.9	90.0
2	NA	13	11	24
	%	12.4	8.1	10.0
	Total	105	135	240
	%	100.0	100.0	100.0

Source of Medical Treatment

The speedy recovery of a disease will largely depend upon the source of medical treatment and the type of doctor consulted by the patient. This is especially true in the case of children. As such, during field survey the sample children and their parents were asked to reveal the type of doctor they consulted when they suffered from illness while working. The responses of the sample children on the source of medical treatment in times of illness while working are presented in table 5.11.

It may be noted from table 5.11 that about 73 per cent of the sample children were taken to government hospital when they suffered from illness while working. About 17 per cent of sample children consulted Registered Medical Practitioner (RMP). There are no wide variations between male and female respondent children in this regard. Besides, it was also reported by the respondents that they consulted quacks for the treatment of illness. They gave the following reasons for consulting quacks instead of qualified doctors:

133

1. In good number of sample villages, qualified doctors were not available.
2. To consult a qualified doctor, the children have to go to distant places.
3. The consultation fees were higher for a qualified doctor than that of a quack.

Table 5.11

Source of Medical Treatment for the Sample Children

S. No.	Source of Medical Treatment		No. of Children		
			Male	Female	Total
1	RMP		20	22	42
		%	19.0	16.4	17.5
2	Govt. Hospital		72	102	174
		%	68.6	75.5	72.5
3	No illness		13	11	24
		%	12.4	8.1	10.0
	Total		105	135	240
		%	100.00	100.00	100.00

Present Health Condition

The sample children were asked a question on how they view their present health condition when compared to that at the time of undertaking work before joining the bridge courses. Table 5.12 shows the health condition of the sample children when compared to that while working. It may be seen that a vast majority of the sample children (80%) reported that their health condition was better when compared to that while undertaking economic activities. The percentage of sample children reporting better health condition at present was higher among the girls (85%) when compared to boys (72%). About 10 per cent of the sample children reported that their health condition remained the same when compared to that while undertaking economic activities. The percentage of

134

sample children reporting that their health condition remained the same as compared to that while working was higher in the case of males (15%) when compared to females (7%).

Table 5.12
Health condition of Sample Children as compared to that while working

S. No.	Health Condition	No. of Children		
		Male	Female	Total
1	Better	76	115	191
	%	72.4	85.2	79.6
2	Same	16	9	25
	%	15.2	6.7	10.4
3	NA	13	11	24
	%	12.4	8.1	10.0
	Total	105	135	240
	%	100.0	100.0	100.0

Leisure Time Activities while Working

The mental and physical development of child depends upon the leisure time activities undertaken by them, while they were working. Free time activity undertaken by sample children before and after completion of their work as reported by them is given in table 5.13.

Table 5.13 indicates that a majority of the sample children both among males and females spent free time by playing with their friends. To be precise, about 60 per cent of male and 59 per cent of female children spent their leisure time by playing with their friends, the average for all the sample children being 59 per cent. About 34 per cent of the sample children helped their parents in doing household work during their leisure time, such a percentage being slightly higher among females (35%) when compared to males (33%). About 7 per cent of the sample children both

135

among males and females spent their leisure time by watching TV. Thus, most of the sample children either played with their friends or helped their parents in performing different household chores during their leisure time.

Table: 5.13
Leisure time Activity for the Sample Children while working

S. No.	Free time Activity		No. of Children		
			Male	Female	Total
1	Helping Parents in Household Work		35	47	82
		%	33.3	34.8	34.2
2	Playing with Friends		63	79	142
		%	60.0	58.5	59.2
3	Watching TV		7	9	16
		%	6.7	6.7	6.7
	Total		105	135	240
		%	100.0	100.0	100.0

Employer's Treatment while Working

The continuity of children in work will largely depend upon the attitude of employer towards them. Table 5.14 shows the nature of treatment of the Employers towards the sample children while they were working.

Table 5.14
Employer's Treatment towards the Sample Children while working

S. No.	Nature of Treatment	No. of Children		
		Male	Female	Total
1	Good	46	49	95
	%	43.8	36.3	39.6
2	Not Good	59	86	145
	%	56.2	63.7	60.4
	Total	105	135	240
	%	100.00	100.00	100.00

Table 5.14 reveals that in case of a majority of the sample children, the employer's attitude towards children was not good. About 64 per cent of female and 56 per cent of male sample children reported that the employer's treatment towards them was not good while they were working. On the other hand, about 44 per cent of male children and 36 per cent female children expressed the opinion that their employer's attitude towards them was good while working. On the whole, a majority (60%) of the sample children opined that their employer's treatment or attitude towards them was not good while were working. The employers were mostly interested in getting cheap labour from the children and thereby exploitative in nature. Therefore, they looked at the children as work machines and not as human beings.

PROCESS OF MAINSTREAMING SAMPLE CHILDREN

In this section, an attempt is made to capture the process of mainstreaming the sample children into formal schooling system by eliciting their responses with regard to willingness to go back to school, whether anybody motivated them to go back to school, year of enrolment in bridge courses, nature of bridge course centres, facilities availed at the bridge course centres,

137

satisfaction with the facilities made available, syllabus of the bridge course, type of formal schools in which they were admitted and their present schooling status.

Willingness to go back to School

The sample children were asked a question on whether they felt at any time after dropping out from school to go back to school. It was further probed whether they were interested to go back to school, leaving their present work. Table 5.15 shows the willingness of the sample children to go back to school. It could be seen from table 5.15 that only 40 per cent of the sample children said that they were willing to go back to school, such a percentage being higher among the males (45%) when compared to females (36%). On the other hand, nearly half of sample children did not express willingness nor showed any interest to go back to school. The reasons given by them were as follows:

1) They expressed the fear that "even if 'we' re-join the school we cannot compete with the regular students".

2) The economic position of the family would not allow continuing education.

Thus, these children had apprehensions about coping with the existing syllabus and competing with other students in the event of their re-joining the school. They also had apprehensions on whether the economic position of the family would allow them to continue in school. Both these reasons seemed to be genuine. About 11 per cent of the sample children said that they could not come to a decision in this regard.

Table 5.15
Sample Children's Willingness to go back to School

S. No.	Willingness to go back to school		No. of Children		
			Male	Fema le	Total
1	Yes		47	49	96
		%	44.8	36.3	40.0
2	No		50	67	117
		%	47.6	49.6	48.8
3	Can't say		8	19	27
		%	7.6	14.1	11.2
	Total		105	135	240
		%	100.00	100.0 0	100.00

Source of Motivation for the Sample Children to go back to School

The first step in the process of mainstreaming the OOS children including school dropouts after they are identified is motivating the children and their parents to re-join school. The parents as well as children had to be motivated to prepare them to re-join the school. The official/person shall explain to the parents the main advantages of sending children to go to school. Besides, children shall also be brain washed. As such, during field survey it was enquired about the person or persons who persuaded the parents and the sample children to go back to schools. Table 5.16 shows the source of motivation for the sample children to go back to school.

Table 5.16

Person Motivating the Sample Children to go back to School

S. No.	Source of Motivation	No. of Children		
		Male	Female	Total
1	Government Teacher	33	58	91
	%	31.4	43.0	38.0
2	NGO Functionary	28	32	60
	%	26.7	23.7	25.0
3	Bridge Course Coordinator	44	45	89
	%	41.9	33.3	37.0
	Total	105	135	240
	%	100.00	100.00	100.00

It could be seen from table 5.16 that about 38 per cent of the sample children and their parents were motivated by the personnel of School Education Department of the State, i.e., the government teacher in the respective villages; such a percentage was higher in the case of female children (43%) when compared to male children (31%). The Coordinator of Bridge Course Centre was another important person motivating about 37 per cent of the sample children and their parents to go back to school, such a percentage being higher in respect of male children (42%) as compared to female children (33%). It was the NGO functionary associated with the bridge courses who motivated the remaining 25 per cent of the sample children and their parents to go back to school. Thus, the Government teachers, Bridge course coordinators and the NGO functionaries played an important role in motivating the sample children to go back to school.

Age Proof for the Sample Children

Table 5.17 shows the Age proof in respect of the sample children, which was required at the time of enrolment in bridge course centres.

Table 5.17
Distribution of Sample Children by Age Proof

S. No.	Age Proof	No. of Children		
		Male	Female	Total
1	Birth certificate	25	34	59
	%	23.81	25.18	24.58
2	Ration card	39	45	84
	%	37.14	33.34	35.00
3	School certificate	41	56	97
	%	39.05	41.48	40.42
	Total	105	135	240
	%	100.00	100.00	100.00

It is clear from table 5.17 that the main source of age proof for 40 per cent of sample children was school certificate. Ration card served as the source for determining the age in the case of 35 per cent of sample children. For the remaining 25 per cent of the sample children, birth certificate served as the age proof. There were no major variations between males and females in this regard.

Year of Enrolment

The second step in the process of mainstreaming the school dropouts is enrolling them in bridge course centres in order to refresh them in the subject and orient them to join the formal schooling system. As mentioned earlier, all the sample children were drawn from those who were enrolled in bridge course centres during 2007-08 and 2008-09. The particulars with regard to the year of enrolment of the sample children in Bridge Course Centres are presented in table 5.18.

141

Table 5.18
Year of Enrolment of Sample Children in Bridge
Course Centres

S. No.	Year of enrolment	No. of Children		
		Male	Female	Total
1	2007-08	40	40	80
	%	38.1	29.6	33.3
2	2008-09	65	95	160
	%	61.9	70.4	66.7
	Total	105	135	240
	%	100	100	100

It is clear from table 5.18 that a preponderant majority, i.e., 66.7 per cent of sample children were enrolled in bridge course centres in 2008-09. The remaining 33.3 per cent of the sample children were enrolled in bridge course centres in 2007-08. The male children outnumbered the female children in the enrolment in bridge course centres during 2007-08, while the contrary was true in 2008-09.

Residential Facility availed at the Bridge Course Centres

It is also important to know the residential facility availed at the nature of bridge course centres in which the sample children were enrolled. There were three Residential Bride Course centres (RBCs) in the study mandals, operated under the NCLP in collaboration with local non-governmental organizations (NGOs). The option for residential facility at the RBCs was determined based on the willingness of the children and parents. Table 5.19 shows the availing of residential facility at the RBCs in which the sample children were admitted.

Table: 5.19

Residential Facility availed at Bridge Course Centres by the Sample Children

S. No.	Facility availed at Bridge Course Centres	No. of Children		
		Male	Female	Total
1	Residential (hostel) facility	62	65	127
	%	59.0	48.1	52.9
2	Non-residential (as day-scholars)	43	70	113
	%	41.0	51.9	47.1
	Total	105	135	240
	%	100	100	100

It is evident from table 5.19 that more than half of the sample children availed residential facility at the RBCs. To be precise, about 53 per cent of the sample children availed hostel facility, such a percentage being higher among he males (59%) when compared to females (48%). On the other hand, the remaining 47 per cent of the sample children were enrolled in RBCs as day-scholars, such a percentage being higher among the females (52%) when compared to males (41%). Thus, a greater proportion of boys availed hostel facility at the RBCs when compared to girls. One reason for not joining the girls in hostels was the apprehension of the parents with regard to safety of their girls in hostels, especially at upper primary level when they usually attain puberty. As a result, a higher proportion of girls than boys preferred to remain as day scholars in RBCs. But, even those who did not avail the hostel facility were covered under Mid-day Meal Scheme run at the RBCs.

Opinion on Mid-day Meal Scheme at the RBCs

The Scheme 'National Programme of Nutritional Support to Primary Education' commonly known as Mid-day Meal Scheme was launched on the 15th August, 1995 on nation-wide scale by the Department of Elementary Education and Literacy, Ministry of Human Resource Development, Government of India. In the initial stages, only the students of class I to V were benefited under this scheme, but in Oct 2007 the Government of India enhanced the coverage of the programme up to Class VIII in Educationally Backward Blocks. The Mid-Day Meal Scheme was also made operational at the RBCs for the day-scholars. Those sample children who preferred to remain as day-scholars availed the Mid-day Meal scheme at the RBCs were asked to give their opinion on the scheme. The opinion of the sample children on mid-day meal scheme is presented in table 5.20. Only those sample children who availed the scheme were taken into account for the purpose of this analysis.

It is evident from table 5.20 that more than half (53%) of the sample children opined that the midday meal scheme was not good in terms of their satisfaction. On the other hand, 47 per cent of sample children considered the scheme as good. The percentage of females reporting that the Mid-day Meal Scheme as good was higher in respect of female children (49%) when compared to that of male children (44%).

144

Table 5.20
Opinion of the Sample Children on Mid-day Meal
Scheme at the RBCs

S. No.	Opinion on Mid-day Meal Scheme		No. of Children		
			Male	Female	Total
1	Good		19	34	53
		%	44.2	48.6	46.9
2	Not Good		24	36	60
		%	55.8	51.4	53.1
	Total		43	70	113
		%	100.00	100.00	100.00

Cooking Arrangements for Midday Meals at the RBCs

The quality of food served to children under Midday Meal scheme is influenced, by and large, by the cooking arrangements at the RBCs. Table 5.21 gives the details on cooking arrangements for Mid-day Meal scheme at the RBCs as stated by the sample children.

Table 5.21
Cooking Arrangements for Mid-day Meal scheme at the RBCs

S. No.	Opinion		No. of Children		
			Male	Female	Total
1	Open School Premises		30	48	78
		%	69.8	68.6	69.1
2	Separate Kitchen		10	20	30
		%	23.2	28.6	26.5
3	No Idea		3	2	5
		%	7.0	2.8	4.4
	Total		43	70	113
		%	100.00	100.00	100.00

Table 5.21 shows that about 69 per cent of the sample children stated that there were no separate arrangements for cooking with regard to Mid-day Meal scheme at the RBCs. The open school premises were used to cook food for Mid-day Meal scheme, and hence felt that the cooking arrangements were poor. Only about 27 per cent of the sample children stated that there was a separate kitchen for cooking with regard to Mid-day Meal scheme at the RBCs, and hence the arrangements could be considered good. About 4 per cent of sample children stated that they had no idea with regard to cooking arrangements for the Mid-day Meal scheme at the RBCs.

Source of Drinking Water at the RBCs

The source of drinking water for the sample children at the RBCs is presented given in table 5.22. It may be noted that 42 per cent of the sample children were taking drinking water from Tap. Hand pump is the source of drinking water as per the reports of 23.8 per cent of the sample respondent children. About 35 per cent of the sample children obtained drinking water from pots arranged in the RBCs.

Table 5.22

Source of drinking water for the Sample Children at the RBCs

S. No.	Source of Drinking Water	No. of Children		
		Male	Female	Total
1	Tap connection	51	49	100
	%	48.6	36.3	41.7
2	Hand pump	24	33	57
	%	22.9	24.4	23.8
3	Pots	30	53	83
	%	28.6	39.3	34.6
	Total	105	135	240
	%	100.00	100.00	100.00

146

Toilet Facility at the RBCs

The absence of toilet facility poses a great problem especially for girls to answer the nature call in the early hours of the day. The particulars of availability of toilet facilities at the RBCs are given in table 5.23.

Table 5.23
Toilet Facility for the Sample Children at the RBCs

S. No.	Toilet Facility	No. of Children		
		Male	Female	Total
1	Yes	54	65	119
	%	51.4	48.1	49.6
2	No	51	70	121
	%	48.6	51.9	50.4
	Total	105	135	240
	%	100.00	100.00	100.00

It may be seen from table 5.23 that about half of the sample children reported that there was toilet facility at the RBCs, while the remaining half of the sample children reported that there was no toilet facility at the RBCs.

Television Facility at the RBCs

Watching some programmes on television will enlighten the children. Moreover, the education related programmes in Doordarshan channel were most useful to children. Therefore, the availability of television facility at the RBCs is crucial in imparting learning in a more effective way. The availability of Television facility at the RBCs is presented in table 5.sample schools as per the reports of sample children is given in table 5.24.

147

Table 5.24
Television Facilities in the School for the Sample Children

Sl. No	Television Facility	No. of Children		
		Male	Female	Total
1	Yes	40	40	80
	%	38.1	29.6	33.3
2	No	65	95	160
	%	61.9	70.4	66.7
	Total	105	135	240
	%	100.00	100.00	100.00

It is evident from table 5.24 that only 33 per cent of the sample children reported that television facility was available at the RBCs. On the other hand, the remaining 67 per cent of the sample children reported that there was no television facility at the RBCs.

Opinion on Syllabus at the RBCs

The academic performance of a student depends upon the syllabi framed for a particular class. The syllabus shall be simple and shall relate to the day-to-day activities of children. The syllabus at the RBCs is essentially framed based on the syllabus of the respective classes at the government schools. During field survey, the opinion of the sample children on syllabus was elicited. Table 5.25 shows the opinion of the sample children on syllabus prescribed at the RBCs.

It could be seen from table 5.25 that, about 51 per cent of the sample children opined that the syllabus of respective classes at the RBCs is heavy. About 39 per cent of sample children felt that the syllabus is sufficient. On the other hand, about 10 per cent of the sample children opined that the syllabus is not sufficient. There were no major variations between male and female children in this regard. Thus, the syllabus prescribed at the RBCs is heavy in the opinion of about half of the sample children, which indicates discontinuation of studies by the sample children could be the main reason for this opinion.

Table 5.25
Opinions of the Sample Children on Syllabus at the RBCs

Sl. No.	Opinion		No. of Children		
			Male	Female	Total
1	Heavy		54	68	122
		%	51.4	50.4	50.8
2	Sufficient		41	52	93
		%	36.0	38.5	38.8
3	Not Sufficient		10	15	25
		%	9.5	11.1	10.4
	Total		105	135	240
		%	100.00	100.00	100.00

Type of Schools in which the Sample children were admitted

The third and final step in the process of mainstreaming the school dropouts is admitting those children in government schools in the age-appropriate class. The information on type of schools in which sample children were admitted after completion of bridge courses is presented in table 5.26.

It may be noted from table 5.26 that slightly more than half (51%) of the sample children were admitted in residential schools like Social Welfare Residential (SWR) schools (28%) and Kasturbha Gandhi Balika Vidyalayas (KGBVs) (23%). While the boys were admitted in SWR schools, the girls were admitted into KGBVs. Also, about 29 per cent of the sample children were admitted in government schools, while about 20

149

per cent of the sample children were admitted in government aided schools. Thus, it becomes clear that most of the sample children were admitted in government schools, whether residential or non-residential, while about 20 per cent of the sample children were admitted in government aided schools.

Table 5.26
Type of Schools in which the Sample Children were admitted

S. No.	Type of school		No. of Children		
			Male	Female	Total
1	SWR School		41	25	66
		%	39.04	18.5	27.5
2	KGBV school		0	56	56
		%	0.00	41.4	23.3
3	Govt. School		47	22	69
		%	44.8	16.3	28.8
4	Govt. Aided School		17	32	49
		%	16.2	23.7	20.4
	Total		105	135	240
		%	100.00	100.00	100.00

Present Educational Status of Sample Children

The present educational status of the sample children, as on the date of survey, is given in table 5.27.

It is evident from table 5.27 that about 69 per cent of the sample children were at the primary level, while the remaining 31 per cent were at the upper primary level. There were a greater proportion of boys (72%) than that of girls (66%) at the primary level, whereas the proportion of girls (34%) was higher than that of the boys (28%) at the upper primary level. It was found that 11 sample children dropped out from the local government schools due to various reasons such as poverty, domestic problems, lack of interest of the child, etc.

150

Table 5.27
Educational Level of Sample Children (6-14)

Sl. No	Schooling Status	No. of Children		
		Male	Female	Total
1	Primary (1-5)	76	89	165
	%	72.3	66.0	68.8
2	Upper Primary (6–7)	29	46	75
	%	27.7	34.0	31.2
	Total	105	135	240
	%	100.0	100.0	100.0

CASE STUDIES

With a view to understanding better the living conditions and the circumstances in which the school-going children drop out from studies and engage themselves as child labours and to examine the effectiveness of the process followed for mainstreaming the school dropouts, a few case studies were conducted during field survey. These case studies are presented here.

Box 5.1 depicts how a school-going aged child was forced to work as a child labourer in a bakery because of a large family and how he and his parents were motivated to re-join the school through a RBC. The child has been continuing his studies as he has been admitted in a Social Welfare Residential School.

Box 5.1: Case of a child labourer in a bakery turned into a student

Mahesh is an 11-year old boy, belonging to a Scheduled Caste. He has the parents, 3 younger sisters and 2 younger brothers. They lived in a weaker section colony near Kurnool city. His father is a cobbler and mother works as domestic servant. Mahesh has studied up to 3rd standard and left his studies, as his father could not afford to bear his school expenses. Mahesh worked for two years in a bakery shop. He secured this work with the help of relatives besides the motivation by a friend working in the same unit. Mahesh worked for 10 to 12 hours a day from 8 am to 7 pm. The work could be considered hazardous for him because all the time he has to be near the fire, engaged in baking and frying. He has to work in the suffocating heat near the continuously burning ovens. At the time of his entry into this work, the manager agreed to give a salary of Rs.700 per month. The employer directly gave the salary to his parents. The employer gave him food three times a day. Mahesh stayed in the work place along with his co-workers. But Mahesh was interested in continuing his studies. Due to efforts under the NCLP, he was later enrolled in a Residential Bridge Course centre. After that he was admitted in a Social Welfare Residential School with the consent of his parents. He continued his studies.

The case of a girl child who was enrolled in a RBC and later admitted in a local government school due to the efforts of the RBC coordinator, but later she was forced to drop out from school once again by her father, mainly due to poverty and lack of understanding about the importance of education among her parents, is presented in Box 5.2. It could be noted that the process of mainstreaming the school dropouts has failed in this case, apparently because of lack of proper

152

system to monitor the progress of children after they were admitted into a government school.

Box 5.2: Case of a girl child dropping out from school once again

Sumalatha, aged about 11 years, is the only girl child in the household of 5 members in Peddakaduburu Mandal in Kurnool district. She belongs to a Backward Caste. Her father works as an Agricultural Labourer, while her mother works as a domestic servant. She has two elder brothers, and both of them are labourers and do not attend school regularly. She worries about what would happen to her brothers and family in future. Because of family problems she continued to worry resulting in lack of concentration in studies. She dropped out from school in 4th class, and she had to work as child labourer. Sumalatha was motivated to work hard in order to achieve her aim of becoming a teacher one day. The RBC Coordinator had motivated her parents. Her parents were encouraged to work hard to save money for their children's education. As a result, Sumalatha was enrolled in a RBC, and later she was re-admitted in a local government school. But, after a few months, she dropped out from school once again, as her father had told her that he could not afford to bear the expenses of her studies. Sumalatha has become a school dropout and the efforts made under NCLP have not been successful to mainstream her into formal schooling system.

Box 5.3 shows the case of how a girl child worker in agricultural sector was enrolled in a RBC and later admitted into a government school at the same providing hostel facility to her in a BC welfare hostel. The girl child has been continuing her studies, mainly because of provision of hostel facility along with admission into a government school.

Box 5.3: Case of an Agricultural Labourer re-joining the School

Narasamma is a 12 year-old girl. She belongs to a Backward Caste. She has both the parents and one elder sister and one younger brother. They lived in Gavigattu village in Peddakaduburu mandal. Her family is entirely dependent on casual wage labour. Narasamma's parents forcefully stopped her from going to school and put her into work. Narasamma worked as an agricultural labourer for two years, working in cotton fields. Their parents were not interested to sending to school by their daughter. The RBC Coordinator has motivated her parents to enrol her in the summer training camp at RBC. After that, Narasamma was admitted in a government school by placing her in a BC Welfare Hostel in Adoni. She has been continuing her studies. She feels very happy to join back in school.

The case of a child who dropped from school and took up work in a tea stall because of in alcoholism of his father in order to support his mother to sustain their life and how he and his mother were motivated to join the RBC and later admitted in a Social Welfare Residential School, where he has been continuing his studies is presented in Box 5.4. The process of mainstreaming the school dropouts and child labourers into formal schooling system has been successful in this case, mainly because the child was admitted in a school with hostel facility.

Box 5.5 shows the case of how alcoholism of a parent could force a child to drop out from school and engage himself as a child labourer in order to support his mother to lead their life. Here the child has been contributing his mite for the survival of his family. The RBC coordinator tried in vain to motivate the child and his mother to enrol the child in RBC.

154

Box 5.4: Case of a Worker in a Tea Stall re-joining the School

Mallanna is a 13 year-old boy hailing from a village nearby Kurnool city. His father was working in a rice mill. His father was a dipsomaniac with an uncontrollable craving for alcohol. Mallanna is the eldest son of his family and has one brother. His father deserted his family when he was studying in the 4th standard. His mother is selling vegetables and edible oil in the market nearer to his house. Due to the financial difficulties and poverty of the family Mallanna dropped out from school and started life as a child labourer in a small hotel near the bus stand. The work he had to do is mopping and cleaning the tables and the floor, washing utensils and fetching water from the public tap. He had to work there always under wet conditions. As a consequence, he managed to find out a job in a tea stall, which functioned during night. Mallanna worked there for one year. Mallanna stayed along with his employer, while working. The RBC Coordinator has motivated his mother to send him back to school. As a result, he was enrolled in a Residential Bridge Course centre. After that, he was admitted in a Social Welfare Residential School and he continued his studies there.

Box 5.5: Case of a School-aged boy turned into a Child Labourer

Kiran is a 12 year-old boy hailing from Ahobilam in Kurnool district. He belonged to a Scheduled Caste community. His father was an alcoholic. His father could never keep his job. The family moved from place to place five times and it was always the responsibility of his mother and children to earn money to live. His father had disappeared from home after some time. Kiran had one brother and two sisters. He could not attend school regularly. Because of lack of regular studies, Kiran was very poor in studies. Kiran dropped out from school when he was aged about 10 years, and

155

joined as a server in a hotel. He has been working in a hotel for the last over one year. He has to get up at 5.30 a.m. and start working. Child workers are engaged in keeping the premises neat and clean, sweeping and wiping the floor, washing plates, crockeries and dishes, cutting vegetables, fetching water, etc., working in the hotel. He took the decision to work in order to help his mother. He was giving a major share of his income to his mother to run the family. The RBC coordinator motivated him to join the RBC but he was not interested in studies and therefore did not continue his schooling.

Box 5.6 shows the case of twins (two girl children) from a family belonging to Muslim minorities joining the RBC and later into a government aided school simultaneously availing the hostel facility in BC welfare hostel, but one of them later dropped out again to help her mother in her business.

Box 5.6: Case of Twins re-joining School but one of them dropped out again

Ameena and Shameena are twins aged about 11 years. They belonged to Muslim minorities and reside in weaker section colony nearby Kurnool city. They had parents and two brothers. Their father was an Auto driver, while their mother sells flowers. Both Ameena and Shameena studied up to 5th class and dropped out from school due to financial problems in the house as their father did not give money to meet domestic expenses on a regular basis and entire burden fell upon their mother. While Ameena helped her mother in selling flowers, Shameena served as a maidservant in other houses. The RBC Coordinator motivated both the girls and their parents and was successful in enrolling them in RBC and later into a government aided school simultaneously providing them hostel facility in a BC welfare hostel. But, after a few days, Ameena had dropped out again from school, with a view to extending help to her mother in her business, as she felt that her mother was facing problems in running the household. However, Shameena has continued her studies.

The case studies presented here clearly indicate the circumstances under which the school-going children drop out from studies and turn into child labourers; the important contributing factors that could be discerned from the above case studies include poverty, alcoholism, desertion of family, absence of adequate support from male heads of household, lack of proper understanding about the importance of education among the parents. The case studies also indicate that admission in a residential school or providing hostel facility in a welfare hostel while admitting the child in a government school would enable the children to continue their studies to ensure the effectiveness of mainstreaming the school dropouts and child labourers into the formal schooling system. The case of a girl child admitted in a local government school without hostel facility dropping out from school once again clearly brings out the importance of hostel facility for the success of efforts made under NCLP and SSA for mainstreaming the school dropouts. This case also points out the absence of a proper monitoring system to follow-up the progress of school dropouts after they were admitted in regular government schools.

SUMMING UP

To sum up, it may be said that the OOS children mostly comprised the school dropouts (90%) and the never enrolled children constituted 10 per cent. Most of the children dropped out from school during 4th to 6th class when they were aged 9 to 11 years and above. The main contributing factors responsible for the children to drop out from school include financial constraints, household factors, school related factors and child related factors. A vast majority of the school dropouts (89%) turned into child labourers, which clearly indicates the nexus between the problems of school

157

dropout and child labour. Most of the school dropouts turned into child labourers at the tender age of 10 to 11 years. They were mostly engaged in stone breaking, construction, agricultural labour, auto garages, hotels / restaurants. The working conditions could be hazardous at times, though these work sectors are not strictly categorised as hazardous. Most of them suffered from different kinds of illnesses while working, and they usually consulted RMPs or were taken to Government hospitals for treatment. They often consulted quacks also for medical treatment. They helped their parents or played with their friends during leisure time.

With regard to the process of mainstreaming the school dropouts into formal schooling system, it comprised three main steps after they are identified, viz., motivating the children and their parents, enrolling them in RBCs and admitting them in regular government schools. The government teachers, the NGO functionaries and the RBC coordinators were the key players in motivating the children and their parents to send their wards back to school. Only about 53 per cent of the sample children availed the residential facility at the RBCs, the remaining children opted to be the day scholars. The facilities or amenities at the RBCs were far from satisfactory, especially with regard to kitchen for mid-day meal scheme, drinking water facility, toilet facility and television facility. About half of the sample children felt that the syllabus at the RBCs was heavy. About half of the sample children were admitted in schools with residential facility such as social welfare residential schools or KGBVs, while the remaining were admitted in local government or aided schools. There were also a few cases of children who dropped out from school after they were admitted into regular schools. The case studies indicate that the schools with residential facility would ensure the mainstreaming of school dropouts and child labourers more effectively than local schools without hostel. The studies also point

158

to the absence of proper monitoring system under NCLP and SSA after the children were admitted into regular schools.

References:

Balagopalan and Subramainan (2003), "Dalit and Adivasi Children in Schools: Some preliminary research themes and Findings" IDS Bulletin, Vol.34, no.1, pp.6-15.

PROBE Team (1999), Survey suggests that if a child is unwilling to go to School. London School of Economics, (last accessed on 2011 July).

CHAPTER – VI
SUMMARY AND CONCLUSIONS
INTRODUCTION

The most innocent phase in human life is the childhood. It is that stage of life when the human foundations are laid for a successful adult life. It is the phase when we are carefree, fun loving, learning, playing... A child is said to be the most beautiful creation of God. But not all children lead a happy life except those lucky ones who receive proper care and affection from their parents. There are children who had never enrolled in school. There are many children who drop out from school at a very early age. These children are deprived of basic education required for their socio-psychological development on sound lines, which would hamper their progress in the adulthood phase, thereby adversely affecting their meaningful participation in the development of a Nation.

The phenomenon of students discontinuing studies and repeating grades or completely dropping out from studies before completing elementary level of education is a major impediment in achieving the objective of Universalization of Elementary Education (UEE) in India. Besides, children never enrolled in school add to the problem.

The school dropout problem is a complex, multi-faceted problem, and the decision to drop out of school is a process, not an event. The contributing factors for this problem could be student-related, family-related, community-related, or school-related. While there are many risk factors that indicate the potential to drop out, the presence of these factors or combinations of these factors do not necessarily mean that a student will drop out. The school dropout problem has been continually troubling the primary education system not only in India but also in other developing countries.

The dropout problem at school level is influenced by a series of independent factors namely school

160

environment, prevalence of child labour, age of the child, negative attitude of parents towards education and the need to earn livelihood at an early stage of life among certain sections of children. Family migration and changes in residence are also responsible for dropout problem at school level.

The school dropout problem is primarily and directly related to the problem of child labour. Hence, it is important to address the problem of child labour in order to effectively tackle the school dropout problem. It is also true that effective tackling of school dropout problem results in eliminating the problem of child labour. Thus, an intricate relationship exists between these two problems. Not all the child labourers are school dropouts; there would be some children never enrolled in school. At the same time, not all the school dropouts are child labourers; there would be some children who sit at home. Nevertheless, it is true that most of the school dropouts are child labourers and vice versa.

STATEMENT OF THE PROBLEM

According to the Constitution of India, everyone has the fundamental right to be educated. Therefore, all sections of the population whether advantaged or disadvantaged, rich or poor, gifted or handicapped, rural or urban, male or female, Scheduled Tribe or Scheduled Caste, must be provided with educational opportunities. This is especially true in the case of the children since the Constitution has provided for compulsory education to all children in the age group of 6-14 years. Accordingly, the government initiated efforts to achieve universalization of elementary education. But, a large number of children are discontinuing their education before completion of their schooling even in the present times. The large investments made by the government on education are being wasted. Several projects/ schemes have been implemented to arrest and reduce the dropout rate among the children in the age

161

group of 6-14 years, but have not been effective in eliminating the 'school dropout problem'.

The government of India has implemented the National Child Labour Projects since 1988 with a focus on mainstreaming of school dropouts in the age group of 6-14 years through Residential Bridge Courses in all the districts with a high incidence of child labour. Despite such massive efforts, the school dropout problem still exists in some districts, which calls for in-depth investigations at the grassroots levels to analyse the reasons for this situation and to address the issue more effectively than before. Against this backdrop, the present study makes an attempt to examine the process of mainstreaming the school dropouts, to what extent this has been successful, what are the major impediments encountered, and how these can be overcome to realize the avowed aim of universalization of elementary education in the country.

NEED FOR THE STUDY

Studies pointed out differential access to education or uneven distribution of education across different spatial and socio-economic groups as the main reason for the varied performance of different states in achieving universalization of elementary education. Empirical evidence indicated a sharp trade-off between child labour and child schooling and gender bias in favour of boys' schooling. Some studies made efforts to determine the factors responsible for the school dropout problem in different contexts. Some studies focussed on factors motivating the students to remain in school. Some other studies attempted to identify the shortcomings or constraints in implementation of different schemes aimed at reducing the dropout rate among school children by increasing the enrolment and retention rates. A few other studies addressed the issues of divergence relating to construction of indicators for dropout and methods of estimating the dropout rate.

162

Most of the studies were based on secondary data and attempted to bring out the relationship between school dropout problem and other factors such as poverty, literacy rate, educational status and absence of schooling facilities at the macro level. Not many studies were conducted at the grassroots level, focussing on the factors responsible for the persistence of child labour and school dropout problems and on identifying the constraints in the implementation mechanism, besides the rules and procedures governing the implementation of different schemes for achieving universalization of elementary education. Considering the widespread prevalence of the problem and large-scale variations in socio-economic and physical characteristics, the number of studies conducted across different states and socio-economic groups could be considered as scarce. Further, comprehensive studies analysing the problem from the point of view of children who dropped out from school, parents of school dropouts, schooling system and implementation mechanism of specific projects/ schemes aimed at mainstreaming the school dropouts are rather limited. Very few studies were conducted at grassroots level in Andhra Pradesh, especially in drought prone and backward regions like Rayalaseema. In this context, the present study is a modest attempt to examine the issues and problems in mainstreaming the school dropouts in a backward district of Rayalaseema region in Andhra Pradesh.

OBJECTIVES OF THE STUDY

The study aimed to examine whether the interventions made in mainstreaming the school dropouts were successful and whether the process resulted in eliminating the school dropout problem, in the context of Kurnool district of Andhra Pradesh, where the intensity of the problem was high. The specific objectives of the study are:

6. To study the school dropout problem in all its dimensions in Andhra Pradesh with special reference to Kurnool district;

7. To understand the socio-economic characteristics of the school dropouts and their households, and to ascertain the causes for their dropping out from school in the study area;

8. To examine the role of government agencies and NGOs in mainstreaming the school dropouts in the study area;

9. To identify the constraints in the implementation of National Child Labour Project and Sarva Siksha Abhiyan programme in the study area; and

10. To suggest measures, in the light of the findings of the study, for effectively mainstreaming the school dropouts and to eliminate the menacing problem of child labour.

METHODOLOGY

Being a study undertaken by an individual researcher, it was decided to confine the study to one district in Andhra Pradesh. Kurnool district, which had the highest number of out-of-school children (school dropouts and never enrolled children) in Rayalaseema region, was specifically chosen for the purpose of the study.

All the out-of-school children who were enrolled in residential bridge course centres (RBCs) in Kurnool district during 2007-08 and 2008-09 constitute the universe of the study. The RBCs were started as part of National Child Labour Project (NCLP) with the objective of mainstreaming the out of school children including school dropouts by giving them adequate orientation and ensuring their admission into formal education system (government residential and non-residential schools). Since the reference period of the study was 2009-10, the enrolment in RBCs during the immediate two preceding years was taken as the criterion for

164

determining the universe, because there is not much lapse between the enrolment in RBCs and admission into government schools and the recall regarding the process would not be a problem.

A combination of Multi-stage, purposive and random sampling methods was used to select the sample for the study. At the first stage, it was decided to give representation to all the revenue divisions in Kurnool district. The district had three revenue divisions, viz., Kurnool, Adoni and Nandyal, comprising a total of 54 revenue Mandals. At the second stage, it was decided to choose one mandal from each revenue division on the basis of highest enrolment in RBCs during the period under consideration (2007-08 to 2008-09). The details of out-of-school children enrolled in RBCs during the period under consideration were collected for the selected three mandals. At the third stage, 2-3 villages were chosen from each selected mandal, again based on the highest enrolment in RBCs during the period under consideration. At the last stage, it was decided to choose a sample of 80 out-of-school children enrolled in RBCs during the period under consideration from the selected villages on the basis of random sampling method. Thus, the study covers a sample of 240 out-of-school children (mostly school dropouts) enrolled in RBCs during the period under consideration (2007-08 and 2008-09) from 8 villages falling under 3 mandals of all the three revenue divisions in Kurnool district, as shown below:

Sampling Framework of the Study

Name of the Revenue Division	Name of the Mandal	Name of the Village	No. of Respondents
Adoni	Peddakadabur	1. Peddakadabur	20
		2. Gavigattu	60
Nandyal	Allagadda	1. Allagadda	30
		2. Obulampalli	30
		3. Ahobilam	20
Kurnool	Kallur	1. Lakshmipuram	30
		2. Chinna Tekur	20
		3. Weavers Colony	30
Total		**8**	**240**

Besides, secondary data regarding educational scenario and schemes in India and in Andhra Pradesh and data regarding enrolment and dropout rate in Kurnool district were collected from different published and unpublished records, which include Reports of the Department of Education, Ministry of Human Resource Development, Government of India, Reports of the Directorate of Education, Government of Andhra Pradesh, Reports of Office the Sarva Siksha Abhayan, Kurnool and records of District Educational Office, Kurnool district, Statistical Abstracts of Government of Andhra Pradesh and Kurnool District, etc.

OPERATIONAL DEFINITION OF TERMS USED IN THE STUDY

The operational definition of the important terms used in the study is given below:

Dropout rate: Refers to the percentage of pupils/ students who for any reason leave educational institutions during the school years (in any given grade or level) and did not come back to finish the grade or level during that school year to the total number of pupils/students enrolled during the previous school year.

166

Gross enrollment Ratio: Refers to the total enrolment of students in a grade or level of education, regardless of age, expressed as percentage of the corresponding eligible official age group population in a given school year.

Net enrollment Ratio: Refers to the number of students enrolled in the official specific age group expressed as a percentage of the total population in that age group.

Repetition Rate: Percentage of pupils/ students who enroll in the same grade/year more than once to the number of pupils/ students enrolled in that grade/year during the previous year.

Transition Rate: Percentage of students who graduated from one level of education, e.g., primary, secondary, etc., and moved on or enroll to the next higher level.

Completion rate: The percentage of pupils/students enrolled at the beginning grade/year of the level of education who finished or graduated from the final grade/year at the end of the required number of years of that level of education.

Education system: Refers to the entirely organized and sustained process of providing education to groups of people regardless of age according to their learning needs. The activities, structure and hierarchy may differ from one setting to another. The process of delivery to the learners comes in such basic forms as formal and non-formal by either a public/government entity or a private organization.

LIMITATIONS OF THE STUDY

The study was confined to only one district in Rayalaseema region of Andhra Pradesh, and hence, the results cannot be generalized at the state or national level. The primary data was collected from the school dropouts and their parents by using recall method, and the data may not be precise, despite efforts made to probe into the details. The secondary data collected from various published and unpublished sources may not be accurate, given the deficiencies in the methods of collecting and compiling the data and the loopholes in the administrative system. These limitations may be borne in mind while analysing the results of the study.

SIGNIFICANCE OF THE STUDY

In spite of the above limitations, the study assumes significance as it is based on primary data and attempts to capture the perspectives of school dropouts and their parents on the school dropout and child labour problems. The study also assumes significance as it focuses on examining the implementation of National Child Labour Project insofar it is concerned with mainstreaming the school dropouts at the grassroots level and attempts to identify the constraints in the implementation process. The study is also important as it makes judicious use of information collected from different sources and attempts to examine the success of interventions to tackle the school dropout problem, which may throw light on measures needed for eliminating the problem of child labour. Besides, the study is an attempt to fill the research gap in the field to some extent.

MAJOR FINDINGS OF THE STUDY

The major findings of the study could be summarised as follows:

Scenario at the National level

1. The 2011 Census indicates the existence of 43.53 lakh child labourers in India. The NSSO survey in 2010-11 shows that the proportion of child labour in total workforce of the country stood at 1.09 per cent, being highest in respect of rural females (1.53 per cent) and lowest in the case of urban males (0.53 per cent).

2. Both the Child Work Participation Rate (children employed per 1000 children) and the Child Labour Force Participation (children employed as well as seeking any kind of employment per 1000 children)

stood at 20, being highest in rural males and lowest in urban females.

3. Between 2009-10 and Dec 2012, 4.23 lakh child labourers were mainstreamed in different states of India under the National Child Lahour Project.

4. Between 2009-10 and 2012-13, the annual average dropout rate in primary education declined from 9.1 per cent to 4.7 per cent. The dropout rate, though declining from year to year, still remains a major challenge. The overall dropout rates in Classes I-V, Classes I-VIII and Classes I-X were 40.7 per cent, 53.7 per cent and 68.6 per cent respectively. The transition rate (from primary to upper primary stage) increased from 81.1 per cent in 2007-08 to 89.6 per cent in   2012-13.

Situation in Andhra Pradesh

1. There has been a growth in the number of primary schools in Andhra Pradesh to the tune of 36.4 per cent between 1996-97 and 2011-12, while the corresponding figure with regard to the number of teachers in primary schools stood at 77.4 per cent. Surprisingly, the enrolment in primary schools recoded a negative growth of -6.4 per cent during the same period. Similarly, the number of schools and teachers in upper primary schools increased by 103.8 per cent and 92.9 per cent, respectively, while the enrolment recorded only a marginal increase of just   1.3   per cent.

2. The Government has been making efforts to achieve teacher pupil ratio of 1:40. The teacher-pupil ratio in Andhra Pradesh declined from 1:45 in 2000-01 to 1:28 in 2009-10 at the primary level, while the corresponding figure declined from 1:38 in 2000-01 to 1:23 in 2009-10 at the upper primary level.

3. There has been a steady decline in the dropout rate at the state level between 1971-72 and 2011-12. The Dropout Rate during 2011-12 stood at 15.60 per cent in Primary Stage (Classes I-V) 20.79 per cent in

169

Upper Primary Stage (Classes I-VII), and 45.71 per cent in Secondary Schools stage.

4. Under NCLP, about 1.64 lakh out-of-school children were enrolled into regular/ bridge schools at the state level. About 1.341 lakh of children were enrolled in 522 Residential bridge courses and 3,063 Alternative and Innovative Education (AIE) centres at the state level.

5. Total enrolment at the state level during 2011-12 was 129.81 lakhs in schools, out of which 52.77 lakhs (40.7%) were in Primary Schools, 21.58 lakhs (16.6%) and 54.08 lakhs (41.7%) were in Upper Primary and High Schools respectively, and the remaining in Higher Secondary Schools.

Kurnool District Scenario

1. The total number of schools in the Kurnool district gradually increased between 2005-06 and 2011-12. In 2005-06, there were 3503 schools in the district, which increased to 3902 in 2011-12, i.e., by 11.4 per cent. On an average, 66 schools were started per year in the district.

2. The gross enrolment ratio (GER) increased for both boys and girls in the age group of 11-12 years from 89.77 and 73.46 respectively in 2005-06 to 95.88 and 80.92 respectively in 2011-12 in Kurnool district. Similarly, the GER increased for both boys and girls in the age group of 13-15 years from 58.16 and 41.61 respectively in 2005-06 to 72.35 and 63.36 respectively in 2011-12. Thus, it could be inferred that the girls are lagging behind boys in respect of GER in all the age groups in 2011-12, more so in the age group of 13-15 years.

3. The total dropout rate of students in classes I to V declined from 29.44 in 2005-06 to 14.28 in 2011-12 in Kurnool district, being higher in the case of boys than girls. More or less the same trends were noticed in case of other two stages of classes, i.e., I-VII and I-X. The dropout rates were still high in

170

class I-X both for boys and girls at 53.42 and 61.54, respectively, in 2011-12.

4. On the whole, 52144 children were enrolled in bridge courses out of which 28698 children (55%) were mainstreamed into the formal schooling system under NCLP in Kurnool district between 1995-96 and 2013-14. The performance in terms of the number of children enrolled and the number of children mainstreamed reached its peak during the period between 2001-02 and 2007-08.

5. The micro level survey conducted in Kurnool district to identify the reasons for the children to be out of school revealed that household work, migration and earning compulsion were the main contributing factors for the school dropout problem.

6. The percentage of OOS children to total children in the age group of 6 – 14 years declined from 7.63 in 2004-05 to 1.22 in 20010-11 at the district level, which again showed a marginal increase to 2.17 in 2012-13.

7. The most important strategy adopted in the district was enrolment in residential bridge courses (56.7%) in 2007-08, followed by enrolment in Madarsaa/ Maktab (study centre for Muslims) (32.8%) and enrolment in non-residential bridge courses (10.5%). In 2009-10, the most important strategy adopted for mainstreaming of OOS children was direct admission into schools (30.4%), followed by enrolment in non-residential bridge courses (24.9%) and enrolment in residential bridge courses (20.6%).

8. Funds received and expenditure incurred under NCLP in the district were high during the period from 2000-01 to 2007-08. Thereafter, there was a gradual decline in the funds received and expenditure incurred under the NCLP. This decline could be attributed to a decline in the OOS children to the total children in the age group of 6-14 years, mainly due to intensive efforts made under the

NCLP and partly due to other socio-economic changes taking place in the district.

9. Due to efforts made under NCLP and SSA, the GER and NER increased at the district level in the age group of 6-11 years and 11-14 years from 2006-07 to 2010-11. The dropout rate declined from 30.63 per cent in 2006-07 to 10.26 per cent in 2010-11 in the age group of 6-11 years, while it declined from 39.76 per cent in 2006-07 to 18.68 per cent in 2010-11 in the age group of 11-14 years.

10. There is near parity at the district level in respect of transition rate from Primary to Upper Primary level for all the children and SC children, but the ST and minority children are slightly lagging behind. Similar trends could be noticed in respect of GER and NER in primary and upper primary levels. But, the gender disparities still persist in respect of GER and NER, especially at the upper primary level across all social groups.

Socio-economic Profile of Sample Children and Households

1. The sample children (240) comprised 44 per cent boys and 56 per cent girls. A vast majority (89%) of the sample children were Hindus, while the remaining 11 per cent Muslims. A majority (51%) of the sample children belonged to Backward Classes (BCs), followed by Scheduled Castes (SCs) who accounted for 33 per cent.

2. The sample children households comprised 1207 persons, out of which there were 573 males (47.5%) and 634 females (52.5%). The sex ratio (number of females per 1000 males) worked out to 1106, which is very high when compared to the district average of 988 according to 2011 Census. Even the household size (5.0) was found higher when compared to the district average.

3. The percentage of children aged 14 years and below comprised about 47 per cent of total members in the

sample children households, which looks on the high side when compared to that of general population.

4. The literacy rate of 45 per cent for all members aged 7 years and above in the sample children households could be considered very low when viewed against the district average of 60 per cent as per 2011 Census. Likewise, the male and female literacy rates of 51 per cent and 40 per cent, respectively, could be considered very low as compared to the district averages of 70 per cent and 50 per cent, respectively, according to 2011 Census.

5. About 34 per cent of members in the sample households were engaged in agricultural labour as their primary occupation, followed by 25 per cent in non-agricultural labour and 9 per cent in cultivation. The percentage of females was higher than that of males among those pursuing agricultural labour and non-agricultural labour as their main occupation.

6. Despite the fact that 240 children from the sample households were covered under NCLP, there were still 109 dropout children and 116 never enrolled children in these households. The large-scale presence of out-of-school (OOS) children in respect of the sample households is a clear indication of high potential for child labour in the study area.

7. A majority of children (54%) in the school-going age group were doing some work or the other. It was found that about 41 per cent of children were taking up work on full-time basis, while the remaining 13 per cent were undertaking part-time work, mostly in the agricultural sector.

8. A majority (61%) of the sample children households do not possess any agricultural land. Of those who possessed some agricultural land, most of them possessed agricultural land to the tune of 1-3 acres.

9. About 66 per cent of the sample households were residing in their own house, more so among the female children households (70%) when compared to male children households (60%). About 31 per cent of the sample households resided in government-given houses.

10. About 43 per cent of sample children households lived in pucca houses and 31 per cent in semi-pucca houses. About 26 per cent of the sample households lived in Kachha houses or huts. A vast majority (88%) of the sample children households had the electricity connection. On the other hand, a preponderant majority (94%) of them had no access to sanitation facility and 92 per cent of them depended on public tap as the main source of drinking water.

11. The sample children households were placed low in terms of possession of movable assets; only 35 per cent of the sample households possessed the electric fans, while those possessing Television stood at just 24 per cent and only 28 per cent had access to cooking gas provided by the government under Deepam scheme. The value of movable assets possessed stood at less than Rs.10000 in respect of 70 per cent of the households.

12. Even though all the sample households were in debt, the amount of outstanding debt is less than Rs.25000 in most cases (88%).

Past History of Sample Children

1. A vast majority (91%) of the sample children were school dropouts. It means that they have had access to formal education before dropping out of school. Only 9 per cent of the sample children were never enrolled into the school.

2. A vast majority (81%) of the sample children dropped out from school while in 4th Class to 6th Class. A majority (58%) of the sample children had dropped out from school even before they completed

10 years of age, while the rest had dropped out from school in the age group of 10 to 13 years.

3. The parents and relatives took the decision to drop the sample children from school in the case of 67 per cent, while 33 per cent of sample children took the decision to drop out from school on their own.

4. The main reasons to drop out from the school include financial constraints (45%), followed by domestic factors (23%), school related factors (18%), and child related factors (14%), according to the parents of the sample children.

5. About 89 per cent of the sample children had taken up some work or other, after dropping out from school and before joining bridge courses. The important occupations pursued by the sample children include stone breaking (31%), construction (23%) and agricultural labour (22%).

6. A majority (60%) of sample children took up work for the first time at the age of 10 years, followed by 14 per cent at the age of 11 years and 13 per cent at the age of 9 years.

7. A preponderant majority (90%) of sample children suffered due to illness while performing economic activities before joining bridge courses. The important diseases suffered from by the sample children include chikungunya (38%), malaria (33%) and other diseases like Dengue, Pneumonia, Diarrhoea, Chicken pox, etc. (19%). While about 73 per cent of the sample children were taken to government hospitals, 17 per cent approached the RMPs. They often consulted quacks in times of minor illnesses.

8. About 80 per cent of the sample children felt that their health condition was much better now as compared to the situation when they were engaged in some economic activity or the other.

9. A majority of the sample children reported that the employer's treatment towards them was not good;

175

they tended to be exploitative in nature and extracted maximum work from the children.

Process of Mainstreaming the Sample Children

1. Only about 40 per cent of the sample children were willing to go back to school, while 49 per cent were not willing to go back to school. The remaining 11 per cent could not decide on this issue.

2. The government teachers, RBC coordinators and NGO functionaries were the main persons who motivated 38 per cent, 37 per cent and 25 per cent, respectively, of the sample children and their parents in persuading the sample children to re-join the school through enrolment in RBCs.

3. The source of age proof was school certificate in respect of 40 per cent of the sample children, followed by ration card 35 per cent and birth certificate 25 per cent.

4. About 67 per cent of the sample children were enrolled in RBCs during 2008-09, while 33 per cent were enrolled in 2007-08.

5. Only about 53 per cent of the sample children availed residential facility at the RBCs, while the remaining 47 per cent opted to be the day-scholars.

6. The day-scholars were provided mid-day meal at the RBCs. Only about 47 per cent of the day-scholars expressed satisfaction with the mid-day meal scheme, while the remaining children expressed their dissatisfaction with the scheme in so far as the quality and quantity of food served, cleanliness, etc. The cooking arrangements for mid-day meal scheme comprised open school premises, according to a majority (69%) of the day-scholars.

7. Public tap, hand pump and water stored in pots were the main sources of drinking water at the RBCs. About half of the sample children reported that there was no toilet facility at the RBCs. Only 33 per cent of the sample children stated that there was television facility at the RBCs.

176

8. About 51 per cent of the sample children opined that the syllabus was heavy at the RBCs, while 39 per cent felt that the syllabus was sufficient. Only 10 per cent of the sample children reported that the syllabus was not sufficient.

9. About 51 per cent of the sample children were admitted in residential schools such as social welfare residential schools and KGBVs, while the remaining 49 per cent were admitted in local government schools or aided schools without hostel facility.

10. At the time of filed survey, there were a greater proportion of boys (72%) than that of girls (66%) at the primary level among the sample children, whereas the proportion of girls (34%) was higher than that of the boys (28%) at the upper primary level.

11. It was found that 11 sample children dropped out from the local government schools due to various reasons such as poverty, domestic problems, lack of interest of the child, etc.

12. The case studies clearly indicate the circumstances under which the school-going children drop out from studies and turn into child labourers; the important contributing factors that could be discerned from the case studies include poverty, alcoholism, desertion of family, absence of adequate support from male heads of household, lack of proper understanding about the importance of education among the parents.

13. The case studies also indicate that admission in a residential school or providing hostel facility in a welfare hostel while admitting the child in a government school would enable the children to continue their studies to ensure the effectiveness of mainstreaming the school dropouts and child labourers into the formal schooling system.

177

14. The case studies clearly point out the absence of a proper monitoring system in NCLP to follow-up the progress of school dropouts after they were admitted in regular government schools.

MAJOR CONCLUSIONS

Based on the above findings of the study, the following major conclusions could be drawn:

1. The problems of child labour and school dropout still pose a major threat to child rights for education and a decent life, despite the implementation of NCLP since 1988 and the RTE Act, 2009, apart from programmes for universalization of elementary education, especially SSA since 2000-01, as indicated by a large-scale presence of child labour across the different states of India according to 2011 Census and NSSO survey 2010-11. Even though there has been a decline in the dropout rate and an improvement in the transition rate from primary to upper primary level over time, the drop out rates are still higher when upper primary and secondary stages are taken into account. Thus, child labour and school dropout problems continue to pose a major challenge to the Nation.

2. Due to the implementation of SSA and NCLP, there has been a significant improvement in educational status of Andhra Pradesh in terms of number of schools, infrastructural facilities in schools, teacher-pupil ratios, enrolment rates and retention rates. But, the dropout rate is still high at the upper primary level, particularly among girls, as a result of which a sizeable number of children in the age group of 6 – 14 years are still out of school, mostly among the weaker sections of the society in terms of social and economic status. Most of these children are working as child labourers, which serve as a pointer to the fact that a lot needs be done in mainstreaming such children. Even though the state government is adopting an integrated approach of

178

tackling the twin problems of school dropout and child labour, there is lack of effective convergence with the livelihood support and social protection programmes focusing on improving the quality of life of the households comprising child labour.

3. Although there has been an increase in the GER in Kurnool district, both for boys and girls in the age group of 11 – 12 years and 13 – 15 years over time, yet the girls are lagging behind the boys in both these age groups. Similarly, even though a near parity could be achieved at the district level in terms of GER, NER and transition rate from primary to upper primary level for SC children and all children, the ST and Minority children are still lagging behind and the gender disparities exist across all the social groups. Thus, these trends point to the gaps in access to upper primary and high school education, which reflects the ineffective functioning of SSA. These gaps are related to the non-availability of adequate number of schools within a reasonable distance, absence of measures to ensure the safety of girl children in schools, inadequate facilities for safe drinking water and functional toilets in schools, and lack of control of the government on fees structure in private schools.

4. The performance of NCLP at the district level could be rated as average at best in Kurnool district, as indicated by the fact that only 55 per cent of the children enrolled in RBCs could be mainstreamed between 1995-96 and 2013-14 and there was a marginal increase in the percentage of OOS children to total children in the age group of 6-14 years during 2012-13. Even though the strategies adopted under NCLP were modified from time to time based on the nature of OOS children at the household level, these did not have the desired effect on mainstreaming the OOS children into formal education system.

5. The fact that the OOS children hailed from economically and socially weaker sections of the society with a large family size, higher sex ratio, lower literacy rates both among males and females, a greater proportion of children in the age group of 6-14 years, low asset base and vulnerable sources of livelihood serves as a pointer to the deep rooted nature of the problem and the ineffective implementation of adult and continuing education programme in the study area. The large-scale presence of OOS children in the sample households, despite the coverage of one child each from these households under NCLP, clearly indicates the ineffective functioning of the NCLP and SSA schemes at the micro level.

6. The fact that the OOS children in the age group of 6 – 14 years largely comprised the school dropouts and a large proportion of school dropouts are working as child labourers clearly brings out the close nexus between the problems of school dropout and child labour at the micro level and serves as a pointer to the need for an integrated approach to tackle the contributing factors for school dropout problem on all the fronts – financial, domestic, school and child – because all these factors are interwoven and are not mutually exclusive, and could lead to the problem of child labour, denying the children the basic right to education and decent life.

7. The fact that a considerable proportion of children, especially the girls, did not opt for residential facility at the RBCs and the dissatisfaction of a large number of children with regard to the provision of quality food, access to safe drinking water and functional toilets, and the availability of television facility at the RBCs suggests that the RBCs are run with inadequate facilities, which could act as a

demotivating factor for the OOS children to re-join the formal schooling system.

8. The micro level evidence clearly brings out that poverty, alcoholism, desertion of the family, lack of financial support from male heads of households, overburdening of the females with responsibility to run the household, and lack of awareness on the importance of education among the parents are the main reasons for the school dropout and child labour problems, which suggests the need for women empowerment as an effective means to ensure continuity of education in the school-going age group.

9. The micro level evidence clearly indicates the absence of proper monitoring system under NCLP to continuously follow-up and effectively monitor the progress of school dropout children admitted into regular schools, due to which there are cases of children dropping out from school once again.

10. Further, the admission of the school dropout children into residential schools appears to ensure the continuation of education for such children, as against the admission into local government and aide schools without hostel facility where the children are likely to dropout from school once again.

POLICY SUGGESTIONS

Based on the major conclusions drawn, the following policy suggestions are offered for effective mainstreaming of school dropouts into the formal education system in Kurnool district in particular and Andhra Pradesh in general:

1. Facilities at the RBCs should be improved so as to create an enabling environment for the school dropout children to get motivated to re-join the school and continue their education further. For this purpose, adequate funds must be provided to the

NGOs under NCLP and SSA to run the RBCs in an effective manner.

2. The RBCs/ Special Schools should have better classrooms, improved vocational and educational material, sports facilities and improved health check-ups along with distribution of free medicines to provide quality education to OOS children. In order to have IT enabled Monitoring, the schools should also have a computer and Internet connection.

3. The curriculum at the RBCs should be flexible as most of the school dropout children find it heavy. Also, the syllabus must cater to the special needs of these children so that they find it interesting to continue studies rather than switching back to work.

4. Taking into account the diverse background and skill levels of the enrolled children, the State Government should develop a standard curriculum for the RBCs/ special schools, with the association of SCERT and/or district level agencies.

5. The teaching and learning materials developed for the children in the RBCs/ special schools should also correspond to appropriate classes to which the school dropouts belonged so as to mainstream them effectively into regular schools.

6. The duration of training at the RBCs should be for a longer period focusing on the specific needs of individual children and help them to explore their potential to an optimum extent. In addition, there is a need for qualified teachers, who must be given adequate training or orientation from time to time in catering to the special needs of individual children, so that they can effectively motivate the children to re-join the school.

7. As far as possible, the school dropout children should be admitted in schools with residential facility – social welfare residential schools and

KGBVs – in order to ensure their continuation in school, as most of the children hailed from weaker sections of the society that entail them an admission into such schools. In the event of admitting them in local government schools or aided schools, care must be taken to provide them hostel facility in welfare hostels for weaker sections.

8. The facilities at the welfare hostels need to be improved so that children would be willing to stay there comfortably and safety of girl children should be ensured so as to encourage them to stay in such hostels and continue their studies.

9. There must be an in-built monitoring system within the NCLP to effectively monitor the progress of school dropout children after they are admitted in regular schools. Similarly, monitoring system should be established in SSA also so as to achieve the objective of universalization of elementary education. Monitoring arrangements should be made at the Mandal/Block, District, State and National level for effective implementation and monitoring of the NCLP and SSA.

10. Since the school dropout and child labour problems are deep rooted in the society, especially in rural areas, there must be all out efforts to tackle these problems effectively, by adopting an integrated approach to strike convergence with livelihood support programmes and social protection schemes. Special packages should be provided in the child labour endemic districts in this regard.

11. The problems of working children of the households prone for migration should be paid special attention, so that they could be mainstreamed in an effective manner. Child labour survey should specifically capture migration of children and address their problems.

12. It is also important not to neglect the adult and continuing education programmes in rural areas

and urban slums in general, especially in child labour endemic districts. Adequate funds must be allocated to conduct adult and continuing education programmes in such areas on a regular basis. There must also be collaboration with the local colleges and universities to involve the students in adult and continuing education programmes.

13. There must be focus on improving the literacy levels both among the males and females. To increase the literacy levels in India in general and AP in particular, the governments should concentrate on retention rather than enrolment, especially in the case of Schedule Caste, Schedule Tribe and Minority groups to reduce social disparities.

14. Developing a good infrastructure at the primary, upper primary and secondary schools not only in terms of equipping the class rooms with modern facilities but also in terms of access to safe drinking water and functional toilets is a prerequisite of a good schooling system. This will make learning more attractive to students, which will help in increasing the enrolment and retention in schools as well as improving the quality of education. The SSA should strive to achieve its objectives more effectively than before.

BIBLIOGRAPHY

Agarwal, (2013) "Child Labour in the Diamond Industry", International Labour Organization. pp. 51-53. The New York Times, February 26.

Alliance for Excellent Education, (2007) "The High Cost of High School Dropouts What the Nation Pays for Inadequate High Schools" www. all4ed.org.

Amarendra Das, (2007), "How Far Have We Come in Sarva Siksha Abhayan", Vol – XLII No. 01, January.

Anil Kumar.V (2011), "State, Civil Society and the Eradication of Child Labour in Karnataka", Vol – XLVI No. 03 January 15, 2011.

Anugula N. Reddy and Shanta Sinha, (2010), "School Dropouts or Pushouts? Overcoming Barriers for the Right to Education", National University of Educational Planning and Administration, Research Monograph No. 40, July.

Balagopalan and Subramainan (2003), Dalit and Adivasi Children in Schools: Some preliminary research themes and Findings IDS Bulletin, Vol.34, no.1, pp.6-15.

Basumatary, (2012), "School Dropout across Indian States and UTs: An Econometric Study", International Research Journal of Social Sciences, Vol. 1(4), 28-35, December, pp.28-35.

Bhattacharya Abhijit "Assessing School Drop-out Rate at Primary Level in Eastern Region of India" Advances in Management, Vol. 1, No.3, September, 2008, pp. 5-8.

Bill and Melinda Foundation, (2006), "The Silent Epidemic: perspective of High School Dropouts".

Choudary, (2006) "Special Article", VOl – XLI No. 51, December 23.

Dev Nathan and Ann George, (2012), "Corporate Governance and Child Labour" Economic and Political Weekly, Vol. - XLVII No. 50, December 15.

Dev S. (2004), "Female Work Participation and Child Labour" Economic and Political Weekly, Vol. XXXIX No. 07, February 14.

Govindaraju.R and Venkatesan.S (2010), "A Study on School Drop-outs in Rural Settings" Journal of Psychology, Vol. 1, No.1, pp.47-53.

Jaba Guha and Piyali Sengupta (2002), "Enrollment, Dropout and Grade Completion of Girl Children in West Bengal", Review of Women's Studies Review Issues Specials, Vol - XXXVII No. 17, April.

Jeyaranjan J (2004), "Women Studies Review Issues Specials", Vl –XXXIX No.44, October 30.

Jobin Joy and M. Srihari, (2014), "A Case study on the School dropout Scheduled Tribal students of Wayanad District, Kerala", Research Journal of Educational Sciences Vol. 2(3), 1-6, June, pp.1-6.

Jomo K.S. (1984) Early Labour: Children At Work On Malaysian Plantations. Kuala Lumpur and London: INSAN, the Institute for Social Analysis and Anti-SIavery Society for the Protection of Human Rights, p. 37.

Khatu, K.K et al: (1983) Working Children in India. Baroda: Operations Research Group, p. 69.

Kotwal, N.and Rani, S., "Causes of School Dropouts among Rural Girls in Kathua District", Journal of Human Ecology, Vol.22, No.1, July 2007, pp. 57-59.

Krishna Kumar and Latika Gupta, "What Is Missing in Girls' Empowerment", Vol – XLIII   No. 26-27, June 28, 2008.

Kukreti Manoj Kumar Saxena B.R, (2004), "Dropout Problem among Tribal /Students at School Level: A Case Study," Kurukshetra, Vol.52, No.11, September.

Kundu, (1984), "Tribal Education in India: Some Problems", Journal of Indian Education 10(2), pp.1-7.

Mario Biggeri, Ratna M Sudharshan and Santosh Mehrotra (2009), "Child Labour in Industrial Outworker Households in India", Vol – XLIV No.12, March 21.

Mehta C, (2006) "Drop-out Rate at Primary Level: A Note based on DISE 2003- 04 & 2004-05 Data " National Institute of Educational Planning and administration, New Delhi.

Mehta, Arun C (2008). "Elementary Education in India: Progress towards UEE", New Delhi: NUEPA.

Mohinder Singh: (1987-88) "Planning and Performance. Closing the Gap In Primary Education", Future. Development Perspective on Children. 22-23, Winter, New Delhi: UNICEF, p. 29.

Monica and Kelly Hallman, (2006), "Pregnancy-related Dropout and Prior School Performance in South Africa", Working Paper No.212, Population Council, New York.

Naik J.P (1975) Equality, "Quality and Quantity. The elusive triangle in Indian Education", New Delhi: Allied Publishers Private Limited, p. 117.

Neera Burra, (1987) A Report on Child Labour in the Gem Polishing Industry of Jaipur, Rajasthan, India. New Delhi: prepared for UNICEF, October, mimeo, p. 37.

Nithiya Amirtham S and Saidalavi Kundupuzhakkal, (2013), "Gender Issues and Dropout Rates in India: Major Barrier in Providing Education for All", Educationia Confab Vol. 2, No. 4, April , pp.226-233.

Pal S.P and D.K. Pant (1995), "Strategies to improve School Enrollment" Journal of Educational Planning and Administration Vol. IX, No. 2, April 1995. pp. 159-168.

Peter.S, Raman K.J and Ravilochanan.P (2006), "School Dropouts of SC and ST Students in Chennai Corporation Schools", The Indian Journal of Social Work, Vol.68, Issue 2, April 2007, pp.248-258.

Poromesh Acharya, (1982) "Child Labour". Seminar, 275, July, pp. 18-19.

PROBE Team (1999), Survey suggests that if a child is unwilling to go to School. London School of Economics, (last accessed on 2011 July).

Rani, U.R., "Reasons For Rising School Dropout Rates Of Rural Girls In India- An Analysis Using Soft Computing Approach", International Journal of Current Research, Vol.3, No.9, January 2011, pp.140-143.

Ranjan Ray (2000), Poverty, Household Size and Child Welfare in India, Economic and Political Weekly, Vol. XXXV No. 39, September 23.

Ranjan Ray (2002), "Simultaneous Analysis of Child Labour and Child Schooling", Economic and Political Weekly, Vol.XXXVII No. 52, December 28, 2002.

Reddy V.N (1995), "Gross Enrolment, Drop-Out and Non-Enrolment Ratios in India: A State Level Analysis", Journal of Educational Planning and Administration, Vol. IX, No.3, July. pp. 229-254.

Rupon Basumatary, "School Dropout across Indian States and UTs: An Econometric Study", International Research Journal of Social Sciences, Vol. 1, No.4, December 2012, pp 28-35.

Sarada Balagopalan, (2004), "Free and Compulsory Education Bill, 2004", Vol – XXXIX No. 32, August 07, 2004.

Saravanan, (2002) "Women's Employment and Reduction of Child Labour", Economic and Political Weekly, Vol. XXXVII No. 52, December 28.

Satadru Sikdar (2012), and Anit N Mukherjee, "Enrolment and Dropout Rate in School   Education", Vol – XLVII No.01, January 07.

Subrahmanyam (1986), "Problems of School Dropouts: A Study with Special Reference to SC and ST in Andhra Pradesh", Education Quarterly, 38(3), pp.28-32.

Usha (2007), "How High are Drop-out Rates in India?", Economic and Political Weekly March 17, p.982.

Venkata Narayana.M (2009), "Out of school children: Child labourers or educationally deprived" , Economic and Political Weekly, vol 39, No 38 p 4219.

Venkatanarayana. M (2004), "Out-of-School Children", Vol,XXXIX No.38, September.

www.ingramcontent.com/pod-product-compliance
Lightning Source LLC
Chambersburg PA
CBHW060256290526
45789CB00001B/334